PRODUCTION

MY BLOG; IGNORED!

2013

WRITE BECAUSE YOU HAVE SOMETHING TO SAY!

By Rich Hand

THIS BOOK IS DEDICATED TO MY MOM WHO DIED IN MAY 2012. SHE INSPIRED ME BY ALWAYS LISTENING AND OFFERING WORDS OF ENCOURAGEMENT. SHE NEVER DOUBTED MY WORTH TO THE WORLD EVEN WHEN I DID. SHE IS MISSED BUT REMAINS MY GREATEST FAN. THE ONLY DIFFERENCE IS SHE NOW WATCHES OVER ME FROM THE BEST SEATS IN THE HOUSE!

INTRODUCTION

I have decided to compile my 2013 Blog as a follow-up to "My Blog; Ignored! This will give you an idea of what I felt compelled to write about in 2013. It is the year following an extremely disappointing 2012 presidential election. I actually stopped writing for a bit and thought that it may impact my search for a new career position.

Most of the book chronicles the political happenings of the day and my take on those happenings. This is part of my "Ignored!" series and I don't expect you to read these words anyway. But in the event you do Thanks!!

There are a lot of lessons in this book that I think are valuable. There are a lot of entries that highlight my frustrations but in most entries there is a nugget or two that may stay with you. If you have a student that is interested in Political Science this book along with The Teenager's Guide to Life, Liberty, and the Pursuit of Happiness: A Parent's Gift!, will guarantee them an A in the course.

This makes a great gift for the Liberal Left Wing Loon in your life! Drive them crazy by giving them a gift that will drive them batty! (This is my marketing campaign. I hope it's not so obvious!)

Enjoy the 2013 postings of my life as a Political Blogger!

THIS IS WHO I AM!... 3/26/2013

I shut down my blog when I started to realize I may need to start searching for a new career. That is a different story for another day. I was advised that if people disagreed with my political arguments it could limit my opportunities to be hired. Makes sense I guess. I rarely talk politics at work but have opinions on politics that I believe are in line with why we are exceptional as a country. I want to help people understand why politics is important. I don't want to demonize people but I have to call stupid, stupid, when it is stupid. For example, thinking that borrowing and printing money out of thin air is sound economic policy.

Most people are not "stupid" but they don't think their political thoughts through. I am here to help make politics understandable for the casual observer of politics. Or maybe I just have to write my thoughts because that is who I am. I am a student of human behavior which is at the foundation of our constitution and success as a country. I must teach and write my opinions. If I lose a career opportunity because of my passion so be it.

So if you are interested in hiring me know this: I am a strategic thinker that believes politics is at the core of keeping our future secure. Politics impacts everything including business. I will not talk politics at work unless it is an environment that encourages it. But I will never remain silent when information is incorrect. I will be who I am and that means being a productive customer focused executive and political blogger.

I have felt something was missing in my life the past few months, and as I feverishly write this blog I now know what it is. I was holding back a piece of me that is what makes me tick in many ways. I have written hundreds of blog posts and articles, six books, three musical CD's, and I now know that if I am not writing songs or blogs about politics, I am not being me. I must be honest with myself, and although I appreciate the advice to stay away from politics, it is not who I am.

So today I am beginning my blog after months of hiatus. It is part of who I am and I will not apologize for it. If the people that hire people don't want to consider people that have a political opinion that is their choice. We live in a free country for now. But a note to those individuals: just because people don't have a political blog or discuss politics doesn't mean they aren't political. They are just afraid to be labeled in a negative way.

Being political does not define a person into a certain category. It simply means they are engaged, and have a true passion to keep this exceptional country exceptional.

I LOVE TO THINK... 3/27/2013

One of the most enjoyable activities of my day is taking time to think. I love to think about the ramifications of actions or ideas often promoted in articles. It can be in business or politics, but I find myself never, ever taking the information on face value. I know I'm not alone but I often wonder how many people actually look at the ramifications of policy.

For example: I look at the intentions of government welfare programs and I think to myself, do the results of the program match the original intent? Having grown up in NYC I have had a lot of exposure to the results of these programs. Section 8 housing was intended to provide housing for low income families. The result was the destruction of neighborhoods, gang violence, and too many people becoming prisoners within their own apartments. Welfare for poor families has led to the destruction of the family. You see, in order for woman to get welfare they can't have a male in the house. They also receive additional benefits for having more children. The result is more single parent households with lots of latchkey kids running around without supervision in dilapidated apartment complexes.

The results of welfare have been the destruction of the inner city and especially the minority communities. There is no incentive to get off the program because the benefits package adds up to more than most people with the same education level can expect from full employment. So as I think about and observe the results I can't help but wonder is there a better way?

Human behavior is easy to predict. It has not changed throughout the ages. You give people stuff and they become entitled. Teach and man to fish and you know what happens? People in America have been blessed with a system of government and an economic system that has produced wealth beyond any past historical comparisons. It has given us the luxury to be compassionate. We want to feel that we are doing something to help the less fortunate so we support any program that intends to help people. But the government is not the best distributor of this generosity. It is the local church or non-profit.

The intent of the new healthcare law was to insure everyone and make healthcare affordable. Who could argue with that? But the results are already being seen and if we look at the track record of other well intended government programs we can predict failure and the destruction of the best healthcare system in the world. All we have to do is think about it. The evidence that the government is not the answer is everywhere.

I love to think. I hope you do too…

PASSING RESPONSIBILITY TO THE SCOTUS (SUPREME COURT OF THE UNITED STATES)... 3/28/2013

The intent of the founders to include a **S**upreme **C**ourt **O**f **T**he **U**nited **S**tates in the US Constitution was not to become a tyranny by committee, but to simply be a referee if the congress attempted to pass an unconstitutional law - or there was a question regarding the balance of power between the 3 branches of government. They are co-equal in power with each branch having specific responsibilities.

The SCOTUS was actually intended to be the "weakest" branch when you read the discussions around the constitution between the founders. They believed they needed the judicial branch just like a sporting event needs a referee (they didn't use this argument but it is the easiest way for me to explain). The rules are defined and provide the guidelines for the game. When there are disputes or the players on the team break the rules the referee reviews the action based on the rules of the game. The constitution is the rules of the government and the SCOTUS is the referee.

The SCOTUS has too often become a tool for those that can't get legislation passed in their favor through the legislative process. The most famous case is Row V Wade. The SCOTUS created a right in the constitution that had never existed before. Instead of allowing the debate about legal abortion to play out in the states, they ruled and created a "law" that has been a divisive issue since. Creating law is not the responsibility of the SCOTUS. Ruling on whether a law is constitutional is.

If a law is not constitutional it is struck down and the legislature can amend and change the law to be constitutional. If it is constitutional the law stands.

The way the SCOTUS is being utilized in modern times is to give 9 unelected, lifetime-tenured judges, the same power as a dictator. It is tyranny by committee. Worshiping the decisions of the SCOTUS is unhealthy and it was never the intent of the founders for the SCOTUS to be so powerful. The reason the founders placed the power to make and change laws in the House because it is closest to the people, and held accountable to elections every two years.

Lawyers love to put faith in the judicial branch because it increases their power and relevance but that is to the detriment of the people...

UNDER ATTACK... 4/01/2013

Why does it seem the federal government is attacking the people they work for? Is it because they are?

Whether it's our constitutional rights, the ability to start a business, or the decision to select a doctor, our freedoms and choices are being destroyed by the federal government. We seem to have elected a group of people that have never had to work a day in their lives and they seem to think that money can be produced out of thin air. We are being represented by anti-capitalist, over educated, and common sense deficient but definitely self-interested politicians.

There isn't an area of our lives that politicians at the federal level don't feel compelled to intrude on even when the constitution is absolutely clear on their responsibilities. But it isn't the constitution's fault for the betrayal that has been conducted on its tenets. It is us, the citizen that is allowing this attack on our rights.

The constitution can only protect us if we are willing to protect it. We do that by electing people that are truly committed to its founding intent. Taking an oath is not enough. The oath has become meaningless words spewed by politicians that have no idea why it was created never mind ever reading it. We have two parties that have lost their way and have forgotten who is actually in charge; the people.

The regulatory bodies created at the federal level are passing laws without the people's consent. The EPA is stopping business at an alarming rate under the guise of protecting the environment. Their true intent is to destroy capitalism. There are too many agencies and every one of them must be trimmed or eliminated. Many of these agencies are acting unconstitutionally. Many are engaging in campaigns to destroy our economic opportunities and the future of the greatest economic system in the world. And our response to these attacks?

Our healthcare system is being attacked by the bureaucracy of the Affordable Care Act. How can you operate under the oppression of 21,000 pages of loosely defined regulations deigned to command and control private people and businesses in the healthcare industry? The reason we have seen rising costs is the introduction of the federal government into the fabric of what was once a completely private industry. Healthcare cannot be a right because it requires someone else to provide it. Think about that. A right is inherent in our being human like freedom. The freedom to speak is a right, the freedom to protect ourselves is a right, and the freedom to conduct commerce between each other is a right. We need to discern rights, wants, and unconstitutional dictates. The freedom to live our lives without government intrusion is a right. Every one of our rights will remain under attack as long as we allow the federal government (and all government) to grow.

Every day we make choices. Every day those choices are under attack. What we eat, what we buy, how we raise our children, what faith we believe in, are all under attack by government. They are under attack because government is too big and growing. The way we stop the attack is to defund and limit the federal government. The constitution is our weapon to dismantle this ever growing campaign to infringe on our rights. It is up to us to take back the responsibility we have allowed the federal government to take from us.

GOVERNMENT SUBSIDIES EXPLAINED... 4/04/2013

The federal government has been subsidizing industries for many years and they are often the target for elimination but rarely are the critics successful but why? Let's look at the industry that is the biggest target for eliminated subsidies; big oil.

The three major categories that big oil receives subsidies for are the strategic oil reserve, farm equipment subsidies, and low income fuel assistance programs, totaling 2.5 billion a year. Oil companies are subsidized by the federal government to put aside a specific amount of oil into the Strategic Oil Reserve to ensure in the case of a crisis our government has access to a large enough inventory to manage a crisis. Farming subsidies are probably the oldest of all federal subsidies. As part of that subsidy, oil companies receive just under a billion dollars to supply farmer's fuel at a reasonable price. The Low Income Fuel subsidy that helps low income families heat their house in the winter represents about $500 million a year.

So when we talk about subsidies for "Big Oil", these are the three biggest subsidies the oil companies receive. The average person hears subsidies to big oil and they believe it is simply money that goes in the pocket of big oil companies but the pockets it is going into is DOD (government), Farmers, and Low income citizens. That is why these programs survive. If they were truly just tax breaks going into the executives of big oil they would have been stopped long ago. Most people don't have the attention span to listen to the entire argument so it is easy for politics to be injected into the arguments. So "Big Oil" remains the bad guy "screwing" the tax payer but are they?

I am against federal government subsidies. The venture capital market is the best avenue for investment in promising technology, products, drugs, etc... If an idea or product is viable it will attract private capital. The "renewable energy" business is the perfect example of why I am against federal subsidies. My biggest concern is the federal government picking winners and losers. What expertise do these bureaucrats have to make that decision compared to private capital? If windmills (which is an ancient and ineffective technology) are a viable energy source- why wouldn't it attract private capital? Because private capital looks at all of the factors including longevity and ROI which they have determined not to risk their own capital. So why risk the tax payer's capital? What does the country have to gain? Sustainable energy? Really, if that was the case why then not invest private capital?

The companies most likely to get federal subsidies are companies that donate to political candidates. It gives them access and unfair advantage. It is also important to remember that it is easy to spend other people's money when the people's money you are spending is not aware of how it's being used. Private capital ventures have to guarantee a return or they will not attract new investors.

The market is the best mechanism to flush out future products and industries. Subsidies are attractive to politicians because it gives them power to control. That is not why we have a federal government. The founders knew that the federal government's role was to ensure foreigners did not attack us, and that commerce was consistently practiced between the states. The constitution was the law and the courts were the referees. Everything else was up to the states and people. We need to move closer to the founding intent...

AMERICA IS DYING... 4/05/2013

90 Million Americans Not Working.

In March 80,000, 600,000, and 80,000 are the three important numbers to know. 80K were added to the disability roles, 600,000 left the workforce completely discouraged, and 80K jobs were created. The real unemployment number is 15% but the reported number is 7.6%.

America is on an unsustainable path. 90 million Americans are not working. We have an employment participation rate back to 1979 levels of 63.3%.

This is so much bigger than Obama. It is time to think about our country again. The bigger this welfare state gets the faster we will spiral into chaos. There is no economic recovery for 90 million Americans.

I find it hard to believe that anyone can support the path we are on. If there are people that still think that pumping money into the economy, expanding the role of the federal government, and raising taxes on workers is good policy they are too far gone to convince otherwise.

The economy is in survival mode and there are always a few bright spots in any economy but simply take an inventory of the American economy in total, and a very sad story appears to any open eyes and minds.

I don't give a hoot about political parties and politicians. I want every federal representative who has been in Washington more than 2 terms removed and replaced. DC is broken and they are breaking America...

America is dying...

GOVERNMENT FAILURE: THE CAUSE OF CHAOS... 4/29/2013

Epic government failure is everywhere. So is the feeling of chaos. Social Security, Medicare, Medicaid, and all welfare programs have been deemed unsustainable from every legitimate audit agency that has reviewed the programs. We have spent billions of dollars on a new federal agency to protect the homeland and we find out at the Boston Marathon that we were under a false sense of security. The threat is greater now than it was after 911. The reason is we have an administration that can't call out terrorism or the people that are mostly responsible for the acts of terrorism.

The new healthcare bill that was passed in 2009 is bankrupting the country and ruining the efficiency of the greatest and most innovative healthcare industry in the world. Unemployment has been at record highs, but more importantly are the millions of people that have given up looking for work or applied for disability. That number has skyrocketed and is unsustainable. Never mind that it is bad for the individual psyche of the nation. We are printing money as if that is a solution when in fact it is adding to the problem of government gluttony.

We have "sustainable" energy companies funded by tax dollars with the only requirement to obtain capital for that business is being a political donor to the administration in power. Most have gone bankrupt after paying out millions in bonuses to the people that ran them (into the ground). Crony capitalism is undermining the legitimate and most effective economic system, capitalism, by painting all capitalism as corrupt. The truth is the government is the corrupt player along with willing accomplices, not capitalism as a system.

The Middle East is a powder keg of radical activity. The Islamic terrorists hate us more than ever even with this president's naïve attempt to "soften" the rhetoric. Syria has crossed the red line set by the president and the consequences? Still waiting to see how far the president will move the red line back. Setting lines in the sand is never a good idea unless you intend to enforce them. The American people have no stomach for spilling blood and treasure in the Middle East so lines in the sand are just that.

The country has not seen this much depression in attitude and economy since Jimmy Carter in the 70's. College grads move back home in the basements of their parents after accumulating thousands in education debt for a "Fill in the Blank" Studies Degree. There seems like no hope in sight for a better future.

This is just the tip of the iceberg in a list of government failures that just keep adding up as fast as the national debt.

And the President plays another round of golf. God Bless America...

DETERMINATION SHOULD BE UNLEASHED & PROTECTED... 5/08/2013

The economy and the markets have shown exceptional resilience in the headwinds of an out of control spending tornado that is Washington DC and the federal government. Imagine if we had an administration in Washington that wanted the economy to thrive? We would be in the greatest economic recovery in history right now.

Why is it that we continue to limp along instead of steam rolling down the economic highway? Burdensome regulations and an expanding amount of money being drained from productive uses. The current administration has a strong belief in the "goodness" of government and sees its primary role as wealth distribution. The evidence is in the numbers. Welfare programs have exploded, taxes have been raised on the most productive in our society, and the new healthcare law is not about health but rather an effort to make healthcare a right so that everyone gets the same fair but poor care from providers. This government believes our problems are a result of free markets instead of understanding free markets are the solution.

Small and big business alike are managing to squeeze out more productivity from their current operations even with all of this effort to undermine them. So I come back to the point that if we reduced our government footprint and let business and individuals decide where to spend their own money, our economy would be on fire!!

This country is blessed with so many people that are determined to succeed. Most of us have been brought up to work hard and take care of ourselves and our families. If we have a little extra we show our compassion through donations. But we have a generation that has been exposed to the idea that fairness is more important than self-determination and free markets. They have been told that community is more important than individual freedom. They have been told government = community. That equation is dangerous and false. Communities thrive when individuals are free to decide their own fate. Government is not a community it is a necessary evil. Everything government does has unintended and often bad consequences to our individual liberty and economic viability.

We still have a generation that is determined to protect individual rights but I am afraid that the next generations are being wooed to place that determination in government mandates. We must teach individual determination and reject government as a community if we hope to survive as the greatest Nation on earth... We owe that to our posterity...

IS SOCIAL MEDIA UNDERMINING THE RIGHT TO PRIVACY?
5/21/2013

Too many people post too much stuff about their comings and goings, where they are eating, what they are buying or feeling at every hour of the day. I am not going to comment on the way people choose to share their lives because I engage in social media sites as well, but my concern is the message it sends to kids.

The right to privacy is a constitutional, God, given right that we should cherish. We should be able to live our lives without interference from anyone including and especially government agencies and bureaucrats. The right to privacy is as important as the right to free speech which is greatly improved with the advent of social media. Social media has given a voice to so many more Americans, and it has broken the "log jam" of newspaper editors that used to control the flow of information. But what about protecting our privacy?

In Utah, as we speak, a new DOD data center that is being built in the name of security is going to be capable of watching and spying on every American citizen without their knowledge. In the name of keeping people safe, the federal government is preparing to make our lives less safe and endangering our right to privacy. We will be less safe from the prospect of an over reaching and controlling government. I want to allow the government to track terrorists but at what cost? What information will we allow them to gather on us? And from where we will allow them to gather information on law abiding citizens?

So here is my fear. As kids spew their lives on every social network without an ounce of consideration, how likely will they be willing to protect the rights of privacy and our other constitutional rights? Their willingness to share their information may cloud their judgment on constitutional limits. It will be easier for the younger generation to shrug off as unimportant the ability and reality of government agencies tracking our every move. They are so accustomed to being tracked by friends, why not the government? And not only government, corporations and advocacy groups as well.

Between the lack of civics and history in the public school curriculum, the acceptance of information dumping on social networks, and the ability of federal government to track our every move, what will become of privacy? What will become of our nation? What will become of our Constitution? What will become of our liberty?

THIS IS HOW TO FIX THE IRS... 5/22/2013

What is the Internal Revenue Service's function? They are the federal agency empowered to collect taxes from the American people. They are empowered to the extent that you are guilty of any charge they make until proven innocent. The constitution grants us the right to innocence and puts the burden of proof on the government when it comes to every other facet of law. How is it that a government agency can be allowed to undermine our constitutional rights?

First, congress should pass a law that puts the burden of proof on the IRS and not the other way around. If the IRS believes we owe more tax than we paid, let them prove it. Why should it be our burden to manage their responsibilities? Especially when the tax code is a million lines of regulations. We have to go to work and make a living. We don't have time to do their job as well. What are we paying them for? Let them cite the law and where we are wrong, and if we disagree let them provide additional proof we have done something wrong. Let them obtain a warrant and then conduct an audit. If they are wrong then we should be reimbursed for any fees, lost wages, and time we have spent defending their claim.

The IRS is the equivalent of the loan shark in organized crime. In reality they are empowered to destroy people's lives and livelihoods. They can show up with goons and make American's lives miserable. They can garnish wages, freeze bank accounts, and take the receivables in your business. This is too much power for any agency in our government. And it is about to get worse as the IRS takes on the new role as enforcer of healthcare. If healthy, young, or not convinced of the need for health insurance, the IRS goons are going to be the arm twisting agency to force you to purchase a product against your will.

So there is a much easier way to deal with this out of control agency filled with America hating bureaucrats. Implement a flat tax at the federal level like every state in the union. If you make 0 - $50,000 a year you pay 10% of your W2 income. If you make $50,000 a year to $10,000,000,000,000 you pay 10% of your W2 or Corporate income. That's right 10% for everyone. That is fair and that is justice.

The federal government is bloated and out of control. Ten percent of the country's income is more than enough to provide for the constitutional requirements.

The recent scandals are the result of a federal government too big and being run by people that are too casual with the concept of law and order. Let's send the 115,000 employees of the IRS packing. Instead of harassing the business people of the United States, let them try to get a job at one of those establishments...

WHAT CAN WE AGREE ON? 5/28/2013

The political world has created a barrier to real debate on very important issues to every American. It seems contrived by politicians to keep citizens divided all the while they drive the government in the direction they prefer. It seems at times that every political question divides us no matter what the question is so the question is: Is there any issue most Americans can agree on?

Freedom in general terms: Can Americans agree that freedom is important? I think so. I believe if you ask Americans if they believe that freedom is important an overwhelming majority would agree.

Free Markets: The question of free markets is often asked with qualifiers that blur the overall concept of free markets. If you ask Americans: Do you believe that the economy benefits when citizens are able to own and run businesses with little interference from government? A majority of people will agree. If you ask: Should businesses be able to run their business any way they choose without any government oversight? Most people would disagree. America was built on free markets and is wealthy because of free market capitalism. It has been a concerted effort of demonization of capitalism which has led to an acceptance of government regulation.

Government Regulation: Can Americans agree there is too much government regulation? I believe most would agree. Can Americans agree there is a role for government regulation? I believe most would agree. The problem is we have political parties that are pandering to every special interest and every special interest is looking to regulate something that creates an advantage for them. This must stop. Most Americans would agree.

Immigration: Can Americans agree that immigration has been good for America? I think most would agree. Is allowing people that have broken our laws to get here a policy Americans want continued? I believe most Americans want immigration fixed. Most Americans want a secured border. Most Americans want immigrants that are here to assimilate and not to take advantage of our generosity through welfare programs. Most Americans don't want to see children of illegal immigrants kicked out of the country but they are conflicted on the remedy. So why not just secure the border to start?

Gay Marriage: Most Americans believe that gay couples should have all the legal rights of married heterosexuals. Most Americans see this as a fairness issue. Civil Unions are supported by an overwhelming majority of Americans. The definition of "marriage" has always been a union between a man and woman. A majority of Americans believe in marriage as a sacred tradition. Why not allow civil unions the same benefits and leave the definition of marriage alone? The other option is to remove any government benefits related to marriage.

Debt and Deficit: Americans agree the federal government and all levels of government spend too much and therefore take too much in taxes. Americans agree we should spend less and balance the budget by reduced spending. Americans manage their budgets and believe government should do the same.

Taxes: Most Americans hate taxes and fear the IRS. Most Americans support a simplified tax system. Most people believe everyone should pay into the system. When asked the question should the "rich" pay more too many people agree. But with a flat tax the billionaire paying 15% of a billion pays a lot more than a person that pays 15% of $10,000. If asked the question whether or not taxes should be flat a majority of Americans would agree.

There is a lot we as Americans can agree on but it is not in the interest of politicians to ask the right questions. The American people need to reject politicians that don't agree with us...

FREE MARKET HEALTHCARE... 5/30/2013

The future of healthcare is in jeopardy if the government gets a foothold. In order to save healthcare three simple things have to happen to put it in motion; government intrusion must be reversed, doctors need to do what Dr. Ciampi is doing, and insurance companies need to offer a high risk insurance option.

The average family medical insurance plan is now up to $13,000 per year. That's a monthly cost of $1083.00 per family. And let's not forget that most of these plans have a co-pay and deductible that must be met before insurance companies pay the bill. If we look at Dr. Ciampi's price list for services, it becomes apparent that for most families, it would be more cost effective to move from a full medical insurance plan to one that covers only catastrophic care like heart attacks, emergency room visits, broken bones, cancer, etc...

Here is a few of the services and their costs that the Doctor lists. Go here for a complete list.

Office Visit (brief) $50.00
(one straight forward issue. i.e. cold, sinus infection, bladder infection, etc.)

Office Visit (regular) $75.00
(one issue of moderate complexity or 2-3 simple issues. i.e. diabetes follow up, back pain, abdominal pain)

Office Visit (extended) $100.00
(multiple issues and/or a single very complicated issue requiring more time, counseling, and/or coordination of care with other doctors or hospital)

Complete Physical Exam $150.00
(comprehensive history and physical exam and review of labwork for preventive health maintenance)

Well Child Exam $150.00
(age appropriate history and physical. immunizations usually covered by state at no extra cost)

House Call $200.00
(for patients who are homebound or too sick to come to office. extra charge could apply if longer travel required)

Nurse Visit $20.00
(for follow up of established problems such as blood pressure

rechecks, etc. Results reviewed by doctor to modify treatment plan)

House calls! If you figure you get a check-up once a year, maybe some blood work, and a cold or two, most of us would be better off putting the money we spend on insurance toward a catastrophic insurance plan and a rainy day fund.

Most of the prices are reasonable and have actually been reduced because according to Dr. Ciampi, the overhead costs of managing insurance claims goes away and his time and resources go toward patient care. Imagine that! Patient care in the driver's seat again!

This is a start and only addresses the basic healthcare market but it is the real future of healthcare if we want to continue to be the greatest healthcare system on earth. Free markets work wherever they are tried and not interfered with by government rules and regulations...

WISHFUL THINKING... 6/04/2013

Does anyone really believe the Federal Government in the capital city of Washington D.C. will ever reform itself? I have to hold back the laughter, anger, and frustration I feel toward the people elected to represent us at the federal level. Everything is upside down.

The country is being drained of all of its greatness at break-neck speed, and many of us feel powerless to stop it. Conservative Americans complain that the federal government has gotten too big, and liberal Americans complain that we spend too much on the military and "tax breaks for the rich" (whoever they are) but nothing will change if we wait for the same people that are benefitting from a big government to take any steps to reduce their influence.

Elections come and go at the federal level and nothing changes. In contrast, elections happen at the state and local level and a lot changes. State budgets are getting balanced (thanks to conservatives), businesses are growing, and energy is being harvested all in spite of an out of control central government intent on destroying everything good in its path. The state level changes happen because the people have more control of holding local politicians accountable. The further away government is from the people the smaller and more limited it needs to be.

The only solution to changing the federal government is to invoke the constitutional rights of the states. The states are the dominant power structure in the constitution. The federal government is given the authority it has by the states and the people. It is time to wean the federal government off of the power it has become addicted to at the state level by a collection of Governors around the country.

Similar to a drug addict, it is foolish to think the drug addict (federal government) should be given the keys to the pharmacy (printing press/borrowing authority) and expect the drug addiction to diminish. The only effective remedy is a full blown intervention of an outside source to ensure that the addict has a chance to succeed. Any other effort to limit the federal government's destruction of our future is wishful thinking...

WE'RE NOT STUPID... 6/18/2013

There are ads running on every conservative news outlets on both radio and television. They are sponsored by a group called the conservative movement for immigration progress or some other such nonsense. They feature clips of Senator Rubio, Congressman Paul saying how our immigration policy is broken. These ads are funded by the left. They talk about how this new immigration bill is going to fix immigration but it has the same border provisions as the current law.

These ads will not work for one reason: conservatives are much smarter and have a healthy skepticism of government and the media than the left does. Conservatives don't fall for the emotional arguments like the sappy left. You have to have facts to back up your case if you want to convince conservatives to support your position.

The argument comes down to one issue: the border. The border must be secured. Marco Rubio says what we have is not working but why is it not working? Because the federal government refuses to secure the border as the law requires. So why would a new law with the same border provision be enforced this time? Conservatives and every thinking American knows that the border will not be secured and the new law will be enforced the same way the current law is enforced; not! It will be another free for all stealing the jobs from our youth, low skilled Americans, and giving our hard earned tax dollars to people that have broken the laws of this land.

I guess the good news is that the left is throwing money away that could have been used on their more gullible constituents for the 2014 election. I have a message to the left: We are not stupid like the people you normally try to persuade with this garbage...

CRISIS OF THE AMERICAN FAMILY... 6/25/2013

There comes a time when two entities that once loved each other, depended on each other, and respected each other have to face the reality that things have changed. Time can be cruel to relationships and 237 years, although young in comparison to others, seems to have taken the bloom off the rose.

At the beginning we shared a common bond, we made what we thought were lifetime commitments to each other, and we swore our allegiance to always respect the vow we signed. Maybe it's a sign of the times where commitments no longer seem to be enough to maintain a relationship or maybe we have just found new interests that no longer align with each other. Either way it is time we do what is in the best interest of everyone involved and separate.

Our federal government was created by the states to help protect us from foreign enemies, make us stronger competitors on the world stage, and referee disputes among the states, but now it seems the federal government has become the enemy of the people. How did this happen?

The first thing we did wrong was to put too much trust in the federal government. When we encountered difficult situations we ran to the federal government. When the federal government took more than it was sanctioned to in the vow we took, we ignored it and enabled it to drift from us. Even though we knew how out of control the federal government became we kept telling ourselves that it will get better. The federal government would say it was sorry by showering us in "gifts" that we knew were taken under duress but we ignored that too.

So we find ourselves on the brink of disaster with a partner that has become an addict of our enabling and no longer can control its anger and abusive power over us. It is time to act in the interest of our nation by taking back the control we gave up over the years that no longer can be ignored. As it is with any addict we can't expect the addict to cure itself. It needs an intervention. That intervention is the reapplication of the original vows our US Constitution.

To expect this monster we have created through neglect and enablement to reform is not realistic. We must use a tough love approach and although times will be tough as we navigate the DT's, it will be worth it in the end. The children are counting on us to do the right thing is this relationship which is to break the bond and separate until the federal government once again respects our place in this relationship and stops the abuse it has inflicted on the American family.

THE ANSWER IS SIMPLE... 6/27/2013

If you are one of the people that believe our future is being jeopardized by an out of control federal government the fix is simple and laid out clearly in the US Constitution. The fix is the Tenth Amendment. The text is short, clear, and concise:

"The powers not delegated to the United States by the Constitution, nor prohibited by it to the States are reserved to the States respectively, or to the people."

All acts, laws, and dictates of the federal government must be delegated to it in the constitution. Where is it delegated that the federal government should be a pension fund, medical fund, or arbiter of welfare money? Any attempt to justify 90% of what the federal government currently does is tortured logic. There are 18 specific powers. None of them include the power to take the wealth of some and give to others.

The founders were very conflicted in the creation of the United States. They knew that too much central power would turn to tyranny, and not enough central power would leave the states vulnerable to foreign interests and could undermine the ability of the states to thrive economically and independently. It is critical to note that the Constitution was intended to limit the central power of the government. Every argument about the ratification discussed the potential of the central government to infringe on the rights of the individual and states. That is why the Bill of Rights was added and especially the Tenth Amendment.

The founders even argued about the Bill of Rights. Many didn't even believe it was needed because the Constitution was inherently a document limiting central power. It was assumed that the people would hold a central government in check. In the day, it was not uncommon for people to violently revolt against the tax collector or representative of any central authority. Limiting power was absolutely the intent. To think the central government was a means to happiness or prosperity would have been laughed at and rejected hands down. But fortunately for us today, many did not trust a central authority and would not ratify without the Bill of Rights. If not for these ten amendments we would not have the country we have today.

There has been a concerted effort not to teach the founding in context. If the education of our youth included the true intent of the US Constitution and the founders, we would be in much better shape today. The bright side is many people are starting to realize how right the founders were. There is a growing movement to utilize the Tenth Amendment and the process of nullification. Nullification is simply the states and people rejecting unconstitutional laws.

Rejecting unconstitutional laws utilizing the Tenth Amendment and nullification is the simple answer. Once this movement gains greater ground it will take hold. To learn more go to www.tenthamendmentcenter.com. You will be glad you did...

JULY 4TH 2013... (POSTED JULY 1ST)

It has been 237 years since the initial Declaration of Independence. It is a miracle we are still free from tyranny but that has only happened because a few good men and woman make it their mission to protect our liberty.

The natural human condition has always been to be ruled by a handful of kings, tyrants, and despots. It seems like a long time ago but it really isn't. The declaration our founders made was not only an act of courage, it was an act that had not occurred anywhere throughout history in an effort to pronounce individual liberty as the natural state of the human condition. Up until 1776, the individual was seen as a ward of the state, subject of a kingdom, the cog in a society to be used as needed for the good of the ruling class.

Even today, England still holds on to a class structure that assigns future hopes to the status of which you are born; heredity. Even today, the opportunity to move through classes is limited and not likely to happen. The world is still full of places that do not live by the rights we hold to be self-evident. It is where our concept of "exceptionalism" comes from, and rightfully so.

Unfortunately our current President doesn't understand why the United States is exceptional. We are exceptional because we value the individual over the government, we believe that are rights come from God, and we never turn our backs on people that want to be free. We have spilled more blood and treasure on behalf of others than any other nation. That is why we are exceptional. Not because we are rich in treasure, but because we are rich in spirit, honor, and faith in God. We do not worship man, we are skeptical of the will of man. That is why the US Constitution that evolved out of the Declaration of Independence and our founding fathers is relished by so many and considered a miracle.

Our country was founded by a small group of visionary leaders that succeeded in convincing a majority of people that the individual believing in faith and God was the key to a prosperous and meaningful future. At times they must have felt isolated as so many of us do now. But they persevered over the most difficult odds. They knew what they were offering was worth their lives and sacred honor.

On July 4th 2013 we must remember that the US Constitution was a miracle and can only endure if we continue to respect and defend it. We must defend it with all the gusto our founders defended her with. It is the least we can do to protect the last best hope on earth...

God Bless America.

HOW WELL DO YOU KNOW YOUR US CONSTITUTION? 7/02/2013

How do you know when someone knows nothing about the US Constitution or our Constitutional Republic?

They use these phrases and arguments:

"It is a living document": The US Constitution is about as living as the rules of poker. Rules of poker? Professor Walter E Williams of George Mason University explains so eloquently why the "living document" argument doesn't work. He asks the question: "would you play a high stakes poker game ($10,000 ante) with me if at any time during the game I could change or interpret the rules? Say I had a pair of 2's and you had a royal flush, if the rules were living I could change them to say 2 – 2's beats a royal flush now." You see, the US Constitution are the rules of the game and cannot be changed. If you want to change the rules you have to go through a process. That's called the amendment process. It is not easy to do which is exactly what the founders intended. The mob mentality based on high emotion can create an environment to make changes that in the future could be misused. The amendment process takes time and effort which dissipates the emotion over time and allows for critical thinking and debate on any issue. Brilliant!

They reference the "Supremacy Clause": And these people believe anything the federal government does trump the states and people. If the supremacy clause was intended to trump every state law it would render the tenth amendment meaningless. If the federal government laws were intended to be supreme, why would the founders have argued endlessly on how the constitution is a limitation on the federal government? The supremacy clause is simply the tie breaker when there are two conflicting laws on an issue constitutionally granted to the federal government. If the state has a law on immigration and the federal government has a law on immigration the federal law is supreme because it is a responsibility held at the federal government. This was really important at the founding because the states were independent and had addressed many federal issues already in their constitutions. There was bound to be conflicts. This was a way to address these conflicts. Diplomacy and treaties was expressly mentioned in the constitution. Trade was one of the main reasons for this and the commerce clause.

They reference the "separation of church and state": There is no mention in the constitution of a "separation of church and state." People that don't know the constitution often reference this. To have some fun ask them the next time you hear it to tell you where it says that? Don't let them get away with "the first amendment." Ask them to reference the sentence in the document? The first amendment specifically prohibits the congress from making any law to establish a religion or keep people from practicing theirs. Remember they came from England where they had a state church and our pilgrims came to this land to practice their religion. This foundation of people was determined to make sure religion was not forced or kept from them. The separation of church and state came from a letter written by Jefferson. The founders talked about how our form of government needed a moral and God fearing people to succeed.

They reference the term "General Welfare": In the pre-amble it has no legislative power and only a descriptor of intent. In the section of the Constitution where it resides it is talking about the taxing powers of the federal government in context with its enumerated powers. Madison and Jefferson were clear in their letters that this power was tied closely to the activities enumerated and not a separate or general power to spend on anything the federal government wanted. It would negate all other enumerated powers. These guys were way too smart to want that.

They reference only the "Militia" in the second amendment: The second amendment was always intended and argued to be the best way to maintain the freedom and liberty over tyranny. The "Militia" was a local group of citizens that would be a defense against both foreign and domestic enemies. The amendment specifically points out a right of the people to bear arms. The amendment shows the concern of tyranny against both the state and the individual and makes sense since most states and individuals were extremely distrustful of any central authority. There was an understanding of a right to self-defense in our country prior to independence as well as after. Any reading on the subject and a casual look at our recent history shows the absolute understanding of the need and right to self-defense. The Wild West comes to mind.

They reference the "age" of the document: "How can a document written 237 years ago be relevant today?" This is probably the most ignorant statement of all. The document is based on the history of human civilization and behavior which doesn't change. The founders were students of history and politics and used their understanding to protect against the bad habits of groups of men governing over men. Free speech is free speech no matter what the medium; print, pamphlet, or iPhone. Same goes for the right to privacy.

They reference Slavery: "The founders were slave owners." Any study of the Constitution quickly brings to light the conflict of the "all men are created equal" and slavery. The founders struggled with the contradiction but if we look at the context of the world at the time; slavery was a common practice. It was repulsive but also an intricate part of the economics of both the South and the world. A fair look back will help most conclude that the US Constitution set in motion the debate of the legitimacy of slavery throughout the world. Slavery was ended and conflicted with all the beliefs we hold to be self-evident.

They reference "old white dead men": This is always used by angry liberals and usually means they are not worth talking to on this or any other subject.

EGYPT AS AN EXAMPLE? 7/10/2013

The rights of Americans freedom to assemble, and the right to petition our government are engraved in the Bill of Rights. As the President acts unconstitutionally, critics ask: "what can we do?" All we have to do is look to the example of the Egyptians that have decided they are done allowing an elected official turned tyrant to remain in power. They are assembling and petitioning and have forced this individual from the government.

This is exactly what the founders intended for our country. Thomas Jefferson was adamant about the people's right to remove an unconstitutional government. He even suggested that future Americans would be forced to take up arms against their government and he was perfectly comfortable with that sentiment. But it would not take a violent revolution to put an end to the unconstitutional practices of this President. It would simply take Americans heading to DC to petition the government.

The President has been deciding which laws or pieces of laws he will enforce. This is unconstitutional. All of the Attorney's General under the last five presidents agrees that the way this president is choosing to enforce the laws is unconstitutional. He can't pick and choose which parts of the law he will enforce, ignore, or change. His constitutional duty is to "faithfully execute the laws of the United States." It doesn't say he can pick and choose which part of or which laws he must execute faithfully.

There comes a time in every situation where action is the only option. Words, lawsuits, and op-ed pieces are being completely ignored by this president. In Egypt they have no real foundation for the actions they have taken except for the fact they know this was there only course of action. It was effective in the sense that when enough people come together the government must take notice. The numbers are overwhelming when you look at it. Three hundred million Americans marching on DC could get the attention and move this government to act according to the US Constitution.

It is not enough to talk about unconstitutional practices. It is time to march and make our grievances known. It is our constitutional duty as Americans and the defenders of our Constitutional Republic.

What will it take? How do we assemble under one banner? How do we convince our fellow Americans it is the right thing to do? How do we begin? What will be the 21st century equivalent of the "shot heard around the world?"

FAILING OUR POSTERITY... 12/15/2010

Our youth is not being educated to appreciate this country and its undeniable role in making the world a better place for tens of millions of individuals. The critic's knee jerk reaction to this opening sentence goes like this, "if you were a slave or Indian you may think differently about that." I am being generous to the left here because they are usually more emotional and profane because that is easier than actual thought and analysis.

The reality is that the world was brutal, full of dictatorships, cast systems, slavery, monarchial kingdoms, regimes that had little respect for anything but their own power and survival. Along comes America and all of that changes. Do our kids get the real story or do they learn some dates about points of history? The reality is that our education system has failed, and worse, they are delinquent in teaching the American story in context of the world.

When talking about slavery it is rarely discussed that America was a catalyst for the ending of world slavery because of the Constitution and Declaration of Independence. The fact that the founding of this Nation was focused on individual liberty is glazed over, and the focus is on the evil of America owning slaves. To put this into context, we will see a similar fate with the abortion "issue" one day. Abortion kills a potential human being and it has been an "accepted" practice but that is changing. Just as the practice of slavery had no moral justification, the abortion issue is similar. How can you justify killing a potential life with no justification? Time, understanding, technology, and knowledge will make future generations question our moral character on abortion. They will look back at us just like we look back at slave owners and wonder how we could have allowed it. How could the people of the world morally justify the enslavement of another human being? How could the world have allowed the killing of a potential human being?

Freedom and free markets have produced the wealthiest nation on the face of the earth. That is the result of the American experiment. The wealth prior to America was stolen by the government. Although we are moving back to that model in some ways, if our youth understood capitalism and our history, they would be supporting free markets and clamoring for smaller government. Instead they fret over recycling and worry about global warming.

This country is not perfect or is any country perfect. We are human beings after all is said and done. We are imperfect but we have been blessed with the genius of freedom and self-rule. That genius and self-rule is the current law of the land. It is embodied in the Constitution. It is embedded in a document that is currently being ignored and is no longer taught effectively in our classrooms.

We are failing our posterity and squandering their ability to have a productive and free future. And the sad thing is that so many of them don't even know it...

THE ROAD BACK FOR DETROIT... 7/23/2013

Note to the NY Times: Detroit ran out of other people's money. They deserved the government they kept electing. Detroit should serve as a lesson to our youth for future elections. If the numbers don't add up you just can't ignore them. People need incentives to work, not another government handout... Detroit is a sad case but predictable and it is just the beginning. The root cause of Detroit's demise is present in most major cities in this country. Washington DC is doing the same at the national level. It is inevitable if we keep ignoring the facts. It is time to re-introduce the principles of the American Dream... A good education, hard work, and personal responsibility, makes for a good life and a prosperous nation...

It is so easy for people that are driven by emotion rather than facts to opine on the Detroit situation and pity the people living in Detroit. Pity is not what the people of Detroit need. What the people of Detroit need is the spirit and drive to improve their situation. Instead of focusing on the pension plans that were pie in the sky promises from politicians, they should be focused on improving the fundamental conditions that attract people to live in a city.

The city of Detroit has a branding problem. When people around the country hear the word Detroit they think of the once great mega of new cars, crime, bloated unions, filthy and broken down homes, and people that have no interest in improving their own living conditions. Why would anyone want to move to Detroit? Is the future so hopeless that Detroit will remain a third world environment in the former fourth largest city in the United States?

How do you re-vitalize a people and a city? The first thing is the people that live there must want to change the conditions they live in. The second thing is that the city must be perceived and truly be a safe place to be. Crime cannot be tolerated but this will take some time and will need to be proven to the outsider looking in. In the meantime efforts should be made to clean up neighborhoods, refurbish buildings and homes, and people should begin opening up businesses to support their fellow residents.

Once it appears that the people of Detroit are working on improving their own conditions they can reach out to the country, and I am not talking about politicians, I am talking about civic and church groups, to ask for a helping hand. The people of this great nation will be happy to help people that want and need the help. Habitat for Humanity, and other groups would flock to a people truly contrite in their efforts to make a better life.

The one thing Detroit does not need is a bailout. A bailout would be a reward for bad behavior. Using other people's money and work ethic is what put Detroit into bankruptcy. The most difficult part of this plan is the effort it will take to change the attitude of the city from victim to victor. I don't have a lot of faith any of this will take place in Detroit. They have been coddled for too long.

I do wish the people of Detroit the best of luck if they choose to be victorious...

DETROIT REVEALS THE FACTS ON GOVERNMENT POLICIES... 7/23/2013 (YES, TWO IN ONE DAY)

- Leadership: When you have a separatist Mayor (Young) people separate and take their productivity and wealth with them.
- Taxes: When you raise them people flee.
- Business: If you threaten them they will leave taking their jobs and tax base with them.
- Unions: You can negotiate any contract you would like but taxpayers can decide to leave and not support the taxes needed to sustain the contracts.
- Politics: You get the government you vote for and voting for democratic rule for over 40 straight years gets you bankruptcy.
- Education: If you can't read you should not be allowed to graduate. If you graduate and you can't read you probably will not find a job. It is especially true when you have chased the business community away (see above). Education is the door to opportunity and trusting the system to government and union's guarantees failure.

- Crime: It must be punished or it thrives. It is the cancer of all inner cities. Justice must be blind and corrupt cops must be punished. Corrupt politicians are a cancer and must be prosecuted without exception.
- Race: When the government focuses policy on race that race suffers. Race relations improve as economic status improves. Unless you put a fence around a city people of all races will leave based on their improved economic status if the above conditions are present.

Detroit is a preview of this nation's future and it is being promoted by liberal democrats. Will they learn the lessons of Detroit and change their policies?

BUILDING THE ECONOMY "FROM THE MIDDLE OUT" ?
7/24/2013

If you are confused by the title of this post, don't feel bad, you should be. It is the most recent statement on economic policy by President Obama. A President that has next to nil experience in the private economy of the United States, not even a lemonade stand. He is an agitator, and a very good one. He agitates many Americans with statements like this.

Let's look at and analyze the suggestion of "building the economy from the middle out, not the top down." If you look at this statement from a purely political perspective, he is attempting to divide Americans by class and agitate people to blame the "top." The top being the "rich", the rich being the people that create the jobs. This president has no problem with the rich that donate to his campaign, and the rich people he gives our tax dollars to for businesses he supports, like solar companies, but the rest of the "rich" he despises. The people that actually create jobs from the "top down."

"Top down" job creation is actually not top down; it is from "nothing to something" job creation. It is people that take an idea and put it into action which attracts customers to purchase that idea, and then it grows, and the person that started from nothing has something that they need help to keep growing. Whew! Did you follow that? That is where the person that took "nothing to something" now hires people and like magic you have job creation. These people are to be celebrated, not demonized or ignored as the president wants to do in his newest transformation as a job creator from "the middle out." Creating jobs from the middle out?

How do you create a job from the middle out? In the real world the only way that happens is that a worker leaves the current company they work at and start their own company. If the person from the "middle class" steps from that job to take the risk of opening a business, they have now become the "top down." They are the owner, entrepreneur, CEO, sole proprietor, etc…, and no longer are in the middle. Starting a business puts you at the top. That's how I see it and how any sound business person would interpret the President's message of "middle out". But we would be wrong!

What the president is suggesting is that we need to grow the "middle" without the "middle" stepping out and creating new companies. He is saying that the government must "invest" (tax dollar confiscation from the "top") to add people in the "middle" without the "top" creating new jobs. The only way you can do that is to transfer wealth from some other source. There are two choices: the taxpayer and the "top." Both of these choices creates nothing new and destroys the wealth creation you already have. The pie doesn't grow it just gets sliced up in a different configuration. The pie actually gets smaller because the "top" leaves and finds a better country to do business or just stops doing business because they are punished for their success.

This is economics 101 and a class the President obviously failed or skipped to hang out with his fellow agitators at Harvard. Actually it is part of the left, liberal, social democratic plan to destroy the wealth of this nation and put government in control of a failing economy. It is all about power, envy, and contempt for our capitalist, constitutional republic. It is because the left despises freedom, free markets, and limited government intrusion in our lives.

This President is an economic genius for the political philosophy he embraces. He is a failure to the people that love and believe in this country. His term can't end fast enough. I just hope our economy can absorb another three years of this president's attempt to destroy it...

INCOME EQUALITY MORALLY WRONG? 7/29/2013

In President Obama's latest speech, he promised to place all of his efforts on building, supporting, growing, helping, whatever, the "middle class." The problem is that this president doesn't understand how the "middle class" becomes a middle class. A quick side note: we fought to end a class system so I like to call it the "opportunity class." But that aside, let's look at why we in the US have more people in a position to live a comfortable life.

We are the only nation in the world that was founded on economic freedom. Individuals that created things, provided services, and followed their dreams and desires were able to interact with others without being encumbered by government. Throughout most of our early history we had what was often referred to as "Laissez Faire" economic policy. Basically, people could trade and barter between each other to create wealth. This economic freedom is the reason so many Americans had the opportunity to live a productive life rather than a life of subsistence as was, and still is, the way of most of the rest of the world.

Economic freedom within the rule of law is the reason we have an opportunity class. The people that created stuff needed people to work for them. The people working for them learned trades and craft and often went out and started something of their own to create more wealth. Millions of economic transactions between people without the meddling of government allowed for wealth to be created and therefore an opportunity class formed. It is not a stagnant class of people. People move in and out of the opportunity class.

Some people move to an ownership opportunity and amass wealth that enables them to live an even more comfortable existence often supporting charities and people who are less fortunate. Other people of the opportunity class squander their wealth and have to start over because of bad choices or circumstances. But the main point is people working in this free environment have an incentive to keep trying in order to move up or stay put.

When this president talks about a "middle class" what he sees is a class of people that are victims of circumstance. They take jobs and their opportunity is determined by some "rich capitalist." He comes from a school that subscribes to people needing the help of government to succeed. Without the government to take the wealth created by others, these people would starve or remain in poverty. This system and this president don't believe in the people to take care of themselves even though it is the reason we are so wealthy. So when he talks about growing the middle what he means is that by taking from the opportunity class is the only way to make it fair. To this president re-distributing income is how you grow the middle and punish those greedy capitalists. That is the exact formula for destroying opportunity for the most people.

It is why we continue after 5 years of this policy to see poverty rise and opportunity diminish. So the question to this president is how is income equality fair? Why keep growing government when what we need is more economic freedom? Government is a necessary evil. The people in government are not necessarily evil, but the function of government always ends up spreading evil. Poverty, ignorance, hunger, homelessness are the result of government intrusion in our economy. Making everyone equal in poverty is immoral...

OBAMA PHONES: A TELLING TALE...8/01/2013

http://www.nationalreview.com/article/354867/me-and-my-obamaphones-jillian-kay-melchior

Find the entire Obama Phone story here.

It is almost a natural reflex in today's mixed up, backwards world of politics to turn to the government to "fix" things in our society. Whether it's; obesity, speeding, freak accidents, bad behavior, or a reaction to any headline the media decides to put front and center. A man jumps off a bridge, lower the bridge. A woman leaves a dog in a car with the windows down, remove windows from cars. People flush 5 gallons of water down the toilet, make toilets 3 gallons. The underlying question is why Americans reflexively turn to the government to "fix" things?

Any casual review of the results of government programs will tell you; government is incompetent at best, evil at worst. Take the issue of Obama phones. To be fair to this president, the program that has become the Obama phone program was started long ago to bring basic service to the poor so they could have a basic line in case of emergency. It was a program of good intentions which as is common with every government program, but the results? Fraud and abuse is the result.

Since the program was expanded to include cell phones in 2008, the costs have gone from $822 million to $2.2 billion. This well intentioned program is now being completely abused. But why would we be surprised? Look at Detroit, Camden, Newark, Chicago, NY, and many other places across the country that are littered with government programs intended to help the people it is destroying. Section 8 housing, food stamps, welfare, public education, Medicaid, and on and on. These programs have spread misery, poverty, and ignorance in the communities they are intended to help. So why would giving "free" cell phones be any different? Actually, why would any government program produce different results?

The Obama phones that this reporter was able to accumulate without even lying about his status shows the potential abuse of every government program. So why do we keep asking the government to get involved in matters that are best left for individuals, local communities, churches, and civic groups to fix? Is it just a reflex? Or is it that people just don't know where else to turn? I think if we can figure out these questions we can begin to really fix our issues as a country.

This reporter received 3 Obama phones which he wasn't even eligible to have. The reason was that the federal government promises to pay private carriers for every phone they give out under the program. Do you see a problem with that incentive? Why didn't the federal government?

THE GOVERNMENT'S DEFINITION OF "FAIR"... 8/05/2013

What is fair? Is life meant to be fair? Is it fair that you have to be 6'8" to play in the NBA? Is it fair that you have to run fast to be a marathon runner? Is it fair that you have to be smart to get into Harvard? In order to make many things that we value fair, we have to change the rules and then accept the outcomes of those changes.

In order to make access to becoming an NBA player fair we would have to put in place rules like: there needs to be the same amount of woman, Asians, Whites, Hispanics, and Black players on every team. These players would need to be divided into players that are no taller than 5'1", 5'8" and 7'0". This would eliminate the dominance of tall players. We would also have to include a number of slots for people that are disabled. The list of rules to make the game fair could go on for pages.

We could take every institution, profession, and employment opportunity there is and make rules to make the possibility of entry to them fair but the results would all be the same; fair = distributed misery. There is no such thing as ensuring fair outcomes without manipulating the inputs. If you manipulate the inputs it is guaranteed to impact the outcomes in a negative way.

The rules of the game must be fair. The US Constitution is the rule of the game for this country. The Constitution offers a guideline for a limited intrusion into the freedom of the individual. These rules encourage people with exceptional skills, intellect, and drive to become successful without the intrusion of government bureaucrats forcing fairness on their outcomes.

Smart people will always be more successful than not so smart people. Big strong tall people will always have a better opportunity to be a professional sports player. People with a propensity to take risks will always be more likely to be successful entrepreneurs. The federal government can try to dictate that not so smart people should be smart but unless those people apply themselves the result will diminish the institutions they are enrolled in. The federal government can dictate that the NBA hires small uncoordinated people but the result is the NBA will lose its fans. The federal government can give money to people to start businesses based on something other than skill but the result will be less business at a high cost.

You can make the access to opportunity fair by making the rules of entry the same for everyone. You can try to make the outcome of results fair but that is a fool's errand. We are not equal when it comes to skills, knowledge, God given genes, and drive, so how do you dictate success? The only way to make outcomes fair is to distribute misery. And that is something the federal government and all government bureaucracies are really good at... Spreading misery...

HAND'S ON POLITICS... 8/06/2013

We're back! My brother Ken and I are bringing back the extremely popular Blog Talk Radio show "Hand's On Politics."

We started this program to discuss the 2012 presidential election and try to communicate how bad the policies of President Obama were to the moral and economic health of this nation. Although thousands of people listened, the president was re-elected. Go figure? We tried and failed but we don't flinch in the light of failure, we press on and will continue to discuss the political issues of the day and do our best to inform the "low information voter."

As a constitutional "scholar" (I have read the Constitution more times than there are members of Congress), we discuss the issues from a founding context. We will apply economic theory (Ken is an economic "scholar" since he can balance a checkbook) in a way it is easy to understand. Ken will use really simple examples that even I can understand. We will discuss the responsibility of the media in a free society. The NSA and the 4th amendment (I think we scared away our "low information listeners" already!), and so many other issues of the day.

We will make fun of liberal policies and spoof their results compared to intent. We will be as funny as we can in light of the topic and introduce "characters" like "Richie Bag – O – Donuts" (that's me doing my best Bronx impressions & Kenny will play the angry, uninformed, full of confidence in what he doesn't know lefty). We will take the issues of the day and put our spin on them.

We are going to take on some guests but only people we believe are worth listening to like Professor Walter E. Williams (listen here). We will also dig into Mark Levin's new book "The Liberty Amendments" and Mark if he wants to join us. We will do our best to support Mark's efforts with this ambitious project!

Talk shows are a dime a dozen but we have discounted ours to reflect our originality and popularity to a penny for your thoughts.

To our Facebook friends: no need to worry all political discussion will be discussed on the Hand's On Politics Page. Phew! Collective sigh! Please join our page if so inclined...

The show can be heard Wednesday evenings from 7:00 PM – 8:30 PM Eastern.

THE TRUE SEED OF RACISM... 8/08/2013

We all want to associate with people that share our values. It is human instinct, a survival mechanism, and creates for a civil society. The values often include things like religious beliefs, work ethic, educational desires, housing preferences, and economic status. But when people that believe that racism is a motivating factor to the makeup of a neighborhood (like the HUD Secretary Shaun Donovan has proposed), programs like the "Affirmatively Furthering Fair Housing" is born.

This program assumes that if a zip code has too many people of one race then it must be the result of racism. When you think about the logic of this type of thought, you can't find any. I compel you to think about why you live in the neighborhood you do? Is it because you're racist? Or is it because you wanted a good school for your kids, it has a Church you can attend, maybe a nice shopping area, a short commute to work, open space or in the city, and it is a place you could afford to buy a house.

When the population demographics are simply looked at from a race perspective, how do you evenly distribute a Black population of 13%, Hispanic population of 15%, and the White population at 72% (2010 Census data) throughout the zip codes of America as this plan intends to do? More importantly, why would you think that race is a factor in any of it? This is the true reason why the people in the federal government and the left are so dangerous and it is why racism persists.

By trying to force people to live together by simply looking at race, you stir up resentment between the races. The assumption that race is why people live in a particular neighborhood, and then forcing that neighborhood to make housing exceptions in their neighborhood based on race, is divisive. What I mean by exceptions is the fact that forcing people into a neighborhood without the necessary means to live there undermines the economics of the neighborhood. The people that live in that neighborhood have worked, saved, and sacrificed everything to be able to live there. Now you are going to give it to someone that hasn't done the same to get there like everyone else regardless of race has had to do? That fosters resentment. Not to mention the fact that they are using the tax dollars they have taken from you to make this possible.

Whenever you undermine the values that it takes to live somewhere, you foster resentment toward the people that receive that handout. Racism is on the rise in America not because we are racist, but because racists are stirring the pot with programs like the "Affirmatively Furthering Fair Housing" program. No matter what race a person is, if they can afford a house in the neighborhood on their own merit, they will be accepted into that community in 99% of all of the communities in America. I know the liberals and left that push these programs don't believe that but the rest of us know it as a fact.

Racism is on the rise in America because we have a President and an administration that believes the answer to "fixing" racism is by being racist. To look exclusively at race to "fix" and "diversify" a neighborhood is to not understand what makes human beings tick. Common values don't rely exclusively on race. Religious beliefs do not rely exclusively on race. Work Ethic does not rely exclusively on race. Living in a city or suburb does not rely exclusively on race. All of these values are based on individual choices that people make when living their lives. They have nothing to do with race. All races make similar choices when they choose where to live. It is just that race is an easy assumption to make for people that are racist. That is the seed of racism and we need to stop watering it if we want it to die…

GOD'S ASSESSMENT OF ME… 8/10/2013

What if, tomorrow God sent us all a meeting invite with the subject line: Your Life Review, Done by God. How would we react? How would we prepare? Most of us have had our quarterly or yearly review done by our boss or the HR department, but by God? I know it might seem silly but it got me to thinking about my life. And by writing this I hope it gets you to think about yours.

As we know, every good assessment has categories and areas that need to be discussed so that the assessment looks at the most important aspects of what we do in our jobs. But what would God assess? How would (s)he determine if we are achieving success? What is success in God's eyes?

I don't know but my guess is God would focus on three categories; Kindness Toward Others (KTO for all of you metric acronym types), Service To Others (STO), and Living Up To God Given Potential (LUTGGP). I think most of us could quickly make a case for the first two measurements and discuss with God the plan we have to do better, but the third measurement is the one that had me thinking and perplexed, LUTGGP. The first thing that came to mind for me was: what are my God Given Skills? And even though I may not have all of the skills I need to be who I want to be - do I have the potential to be that person? You see, it does start to get interesting!

What do I believe was God's plan for me? I believe we all have a purpose here on earth so we must have been given a plan? Not the step by step type plan but as a pirate might say, "More like guidelines." What would God say about my potential, and have I lived up to it? Would he say, "Rich, I had so many hopes for you, and it seems you have steered away from every one of the things I gave you the skills to be." Or would she say, "Rich, you have really taken the lemon of a life I gave you and made lemonade!"

If something is burning in our belly and we conveniently find ways to ignore it, what would God say? "I have given you the passion because I know you have the GGP (God Given Potential in case you forgot) but you have ignored it. Why?" "I did not place the fear there, you did." "Why do you fear what you desire to do with your life?"

The older we get, the more we seem to reflect on the past. It may be that we just have more past to reflect on, but can it also be that we want to make a positive impact and know time is running out? I am not being doomsday(ish), I just know that time keeps going and we can't stop time. Someday it will run out for all of us- is all I am saying.

Are we going to be ready for our assessment? Will we have a positive tale to tell? The tale can be as simple as volunteering to help the elderly or disabled. The tale could be you're a great coach for your kid's team. It could simply be being the best husband or wife, father or mother you can be. It could be setting your kids up for a bright future, or reading to kids that need help to get to that bright future.

I was just thinking and I thought I would share these thoughts with you. Is that part of my potential? I don't know but I have a lot of fire in the belly type of things I am and will pursue. I hope I, and you pass the assessment if one ever comes... I hope we all get the promotion!

SINGLE PAYER WILL NEVER WORK... 8/1/2013

We are now hearing the true intentions of Obamacare as a "single payer" system. What that really means is the government becomes the only "insurer" of healthcare. Ultimately the government becomes a monopoly for approval of services provided, and the payment for those services to medical professionals which are doctors and hospitals.

The reason it can't work is basic economics. Supply and demand will create two systems: one will be for people that can't afford to pay out of pocket, and those that are willing to pay out of pocket. I will describe the two systems and you tell me which one is likely to prevail.

Single Payer: Under this system the government becomes the insurer and will decide how much the premium will cost, what health services it will cover, and how much it will pay the provider (doctor/hospital) for the service. There is no competition to the government so premiums will continue to rise whether it is through individuals being forced to pay more or some kind of increased tax to subsidize individuals. The individual will only be able to get healthcare that is covered. This is where the death panels come in. In order to contain skyrocketing costs because now everyone thinks healthcare is "free" (demand increases to unsustainable levels), hip replacements for example, will be subject to a government bureaucrat's approval. If you are 80 years old in marginal health, do you think the replacement will be approved? Long lines, doctor shortages, and poor care will be the results of this system. Doctors and hospitals will create a separate system in order to make more money.

Free Market Care: This system will develop because of the inefficiency, corruption; wait times, lack of doctors and hospitals, and fundamental collapse of the government single payer system. Doctors and hospitals will limit the care they provide to the government system or completely drop out of the single payer system, and start an all cash system. This system will work on all of the free market system principles and thrive. People that can afford to pay will pay out of pocket. They will get excellent care, short wait times, and will get any service based on their willingness to pay. Doctors and hospitals will charge what the market, (people willing to pay a price) keeping them incentivized to provide the service. This is the same principle every business works under in a free market system. This is the system we should be embracing now but we have too many people that think the government is a good alternative, especially leftists.

There will be some attempts by the government to make laws that force doctors to provide service to their patients, and laws that make it illegal to set up private practices, but this will create a revolution of types and most likely will be termed slavery, therefore unconstitutional.

"Single Payer" is code for government controlled, socialist healthcare. The healthcare system can't sustain itself with the government in control. It will destroy itself under the weight of incompetence. We already have every entitlement the federal government controls now on a path to bankruptcy. Taking on healthcare will exponentially reduce the time it takes to get there...

COMMON CORE IS NOT COMMON SENSE... 8/19/2013

The newest push for creating education "standards" for the American public school system have taken shape and they are packaged in a program called the "Common Core Curriculum". This new set of standards is supposed to focus on the learning needed to be a success in the world. But when an administrator in the Illinois public school system argues that it is more important to explain how a student gets an answer of 11 from a 4x3 multiplication problem, instead of getting the right answer, this is a program that lacks all common sense.

Anything created by Washington DC bureaucrats (and state politicians associated with DC) to teach our children should be thrown out just because it comes from Washington DC elites. It is also a product of the "do-gooder" types like Bill Gates (who does good through charities) and others that have forgotten what education is and is not. It is not a one size fits all proposition.

Centralized command and control of education dumbs down everyone. Education should be a local process that teaches to the strengths and skills of the individual student. Should every kid know how to read, write, and calculate numbers? Yes, but how they get there is best left to local educators and parents to determine.

Many educated men and women throughout our history were self-taught including President Lincoln. Education is the self-pursuit of knowledge. Our kids need to be taught a passion to learn and what will make them the most productive throughout their lives. By bringing together parents, educators, and the business community, local communities could determine what works best for their kids. Setting guidelines for students at certain levels is fine but to make a kid wait to take calculus until 10th grade when a kid is ready in the 6th grade is ludicrous. The study of the US Constitution and American history must replace all of this global push but that's a post for another day.

Home school programs have the right formula in many ways. Most curriculums are self-paced. Kids are encouraged to keep moving forward and learning more at their pace. When you base education on a kid's age it is limiting to so many kids. Kids are smarter than most people give them credit for.

Common Core makes no sense. We have a 50% drop out rate in many urban public school systems. In many more affluent communities we have kids in first grade that can already read, write, add, multiply and subtract but when the get to school their education is slowed down to align what they learn with their age. How do you create a one size fits all program when there are millions of sizes of educational preparedness?

The answer is you can't. The answer is not Common Core, it is common sense...

THE LIBERTY AMENDMENTS: IT IS TIME! 8/22/2013

I am an avid Mark Levin listener and supporter. I wanted to make that perfectly clear as I discuss his new book which is really a call to action, "The Liberty Amendments."

I have been reading books about the history and founding of our country for many years now. I believe that reading the Constitution is important but understanding the context of when and why it was written is as important, if not more important, for a true understanding of the intent of our founders. I wish this book had come out sooner because in encapsulates everything I have read to date that has provided me with the knowledge to argue the intent of the Constitution. It would have saved me a lot of reading! I am only half kidding because I do love reading our history, but for those of you that find history a chore, you now have the perfect alternative.

Mark has taken what so many true constitutional conservatives have been thinking and has given us a plan to rally around for the sake of saving our future in the Liberty Amendments. My brother and I do a little known Blog Talk Radio program called "Hand's On Politics" and this book is going to be a feature item during our shows to help Mark rally the troops. The beauty of it is Mark has created an easy read and the book is only a few hundred pages. You will not want to put it down if you love this country.

Mark is too humble when he talks about the book as being a "conversation starter." It is a book that is going to create a constitutional movement stemming from the grass roots where it belongs. To think that the federal government will ever reign itself in is a fool's hope. As Mark lays it out in plain words and plenty of supporting facts and statistics, we the people need to take back control through the amendment process laid out so prophetically in Article V of the Constitution. It must start in our state legislatures where we can have a true impact as individuals, and for the purpose of rebalancing the power between the states and her "baby" the federal government.

The amendments are an excellent foundation to restore the Founder's intent. He starts with the Balanced Budget Amendment which is supported by overwhelming numbers of the citizenry and would be the perfect way to "test" out the process for those weary of a gathering to change our most cherished form of government, the Constitutional Republic. The Founders knew that someday the federal government would overstep its founding intent and provided the mechanism to take it back. The state initiated amendment process is also limited in scope to amending the constitution, and must be supported by 3/4ths of the state legislatures to become law. So there is a strong hurdle and impediment that will allow only the most needed and supported amendments to pass.

Mark has laid out the argument and path forward to get it done. I know the Founder's would have been proud but they would have said, "What took you so long?" Although it may seem late in the process, politics often needs the right circumstances to whip people into action. The politicians in Washington have created the circumstances and Mark has provided the plan.

My only question is: "What are we waiting for?"

THE FEDERAL DISCONNECT... 9/03/2013

The federal government is ruining the economy, undermining liberty and privacy, and now considering a military move to "punish' Syria for using chemical weapons. Even when there is evidence that both sides in the civil war in Syria have chemical weapons, we are blaming one side over the other without knowing who actually used the weapon.

The American people have no interest in another war in another nation that hates our guts. When are we going to learn? What is it with Senator McCain, Graham, and now speaker Boehner, that they feel obligated to taking action? They are representatives of the people and only 9% support any action in Syria. Why the urgency? What is our interest? How will a couple of American missile strikes "punish" anyone for using chemical weapons? Needless to say, both of the factions in Syria are our enemies.

We have lost the connection of our representative republic. The Constitution is being trampled at every turn and no one in the government is listening to the people they are representing. The circumstances we find ourselves in are the exact reason the founders created a limited federal government.

It is time to reinstate our federal limits. Mark Levin's new book the Liberty Amendments is correct in suggesting there is no way we can count on the federal behemoth to reform itself. We must take control and reinforce the US Constitution by adding amendments that will codify any ambiguity of the founder's intent. Like a balanced budget, limits on federal spending and printing money, term limits, and a number of other limits needed to get us back on a path of constitutional republic values.

The federal government has been too large for too long and the time is now to rein it in. These representatives will not vote for anything that will limit their power. They have been consumed by the self-indulgent importance in the "club" they have created in Washington DC. They need to be reminded who they work for and what their role is.

We need to reconnect in the political process to awaken the federal government to a renewed constitutional republic…

REMEMBERING AND REMINDING… 9/11/2013

Today is the 12th year to the day of the attack on America by Islamic terrorists. That day is etched in the minds of most Americans, and almost everyone can tell you where they were, and how they felt that day. Most of us (including me) knew somebody who was a victim of the attack. We spend this day remembering the people who died and the people that heroically saved countless others from death.

But where are the reminders? The national media is very reluctant to show the towers on that day as they were struck and later crumbled to the ground. Every time I see those towers get struck by the planes and every time I see the towers crumble I am reminded of the importance of never forgetting there are still terrorists out there determined to kill us. Islamic terrorists hate what America stands for and would like nothing more than repeating the kind of attack that happened on 9/11/2001.

Why do we rarely see the images of this day? Why if they do show the footage is it done so rarely? It should be played over and over as a reminder of why we remember. Islam is a danger to this country and it is politically incorrect to say so. But every American knows that it is Islam that is at the root of the evil that happened that day. It is not a small radical sect of Islam, but rather a very large and organized group as seen in every Middle Eastern country currently in flames. Until Islam goes through a reformation or the people who defend Islam as a religion of "peace" speak out and condemn these terrorists, then Americans will remain suspicious and on guard against Islam.

In order to remember, remind, and survive, we must embrace the truth of the matter, view the images, and call the perpetrators for who they are and represent. That is the only way our future can be secured. We can't put our heads in the sand on what this religion professes to accomplish. Sharia law and Islam are not compatible with a constitutional republic. That is a fact the way the religion is currently practiced.

Today we honor our fallen and our heroes. Today we remind our fellow Americans about who and why this was done to us. Today we remember to stay diligent and honest about what we need to do to remain free and keep our enemies at bay. Today we profess the truth in honor of those who were taken so brutally from us for simply being American...

BLAME THE FEDERAL GOVERNMENT NOT THE "RICH'... 9/16/2013

We are working less because the federal government is squeezing out the private sector. The "rich" are to blame according to the President and his party, but it is he and his party that are destroying the opportunity class and our future economic recovery. There is a full court press by this President to blame the rich and many will believe him but will never see a recovery until they accept the truth. The truth is that the only "plan" he has is to destroy the rich by taking away their incentive to produce through higher taxes and increased regulation.

If you believe the federal government is the answer, you are a significant part of the problem. Until we cut federal spending and intrusion into our lives we will continue on this path of misery. The federal government does not care about the individual. It is a leach that can only survive by sucking the blood of its host, the American economy. It does that by limiting freedom and stealing the wealth of the producers.

We can't wait another 3 years to fix this and turn our country around. The 2014 election cycle needs to change the leadership in the house and senate. It is not republicans that will turn us around. It will be constitutional conservatives that happen to be republicans who are the leaders we need. We also need to follow the advice and guidance of Mark Levin.

The Liberty Amendments, the newest book from Mark Levin has the answer. We need to activate the state legislatures to stop the out of control bureaucracy in DC. There is no one in the federal government that can be counted on to put themselves out of business. We need to do it in the states if we are to survive.

This road will be difficult but the road we are on will be devastating. Stop blaming the rich and understand that the federal government is to blame. It is time to take back control and fix this country. It is up to us and the states. Stop investing any hope in people that are living off the federal largesse. They will protect their largesse with the fury of a cornered animal. We need to start acting like the cornered animal we are...

REAL POVERTY IS COMING... 9/18/2013

The Census Bureau recently released a report on poverty and the reporting on it in the media was predictable. The mantra was the "rich get richer", "the gap between the rich and poor widens", etc... Instead of an analysis of the cause of poverty, and how we could all be headed to real poverty, we heard the typical emotional arguments about the unfairness of some people doing better than others. Here is my analysis.

Let's start with the definition of poverty: *"state of being poor: the state of not having enough money to take care of basic needs such as food, clothing, and housing."* In most of the world this definition applies but in America, most people in poverty have plenty to eat, drink, and have a place to live, have a TV, cable, iPods, computers, cell phones, and a car. So how can this be poverty as compared to the rest of the world? This is not poverty this is income redistribution and an effort to foster class envy. It is also unsustainable, and if not corrected could be the beginning of the end of our way of life as we know it.

The democrats are notorious for stoking envy but the republicans are not exempt. The reason the opportunity class is shrinking is because the federal government is taking the wealth through taxation. The median income is down to around $50,000 per year, the lowest it's been in a very long time. Every dollar the federal government takes from the productive people to give to people in "poverty" the less money is available to be put to productive use in the economy. The people in poverty are getting what would be equal in value to a productive person bringing home $38,000 in wages. Is this poverty? We need to bring back real poverty so people have an incentive to climb out of it. We should feed people who can't feed themselves and provide a basic roof over their heads but everything else must go.

Who defines poverty? The government and that is the problem. The government has a self-interest to increase its tentacles to ensure its survival and growth. It needs to be stopped or we will all be in poverty. Before you say, poverty doesn't seem that bad, the poverty we will all encounter will not be what we see today. It will include a collapse of the financial system, food shortages and absolute chaos which will generate more calls for a government "solution" which is exactly what we don't need. We need to collapse the central government.

The generations of people in poverty are mostly people that have failed out of the education system, depended on government for their subsistence for generations, are disproportionately black and minority, and are the most vulnerable to a struggling economy. They are squeezed out by the educated in society which are mostly white. That is where the dishonesty and racial politics rears its ugly head.

Poverty is the result of poor choices not race or some other demographic. Most people in poverty failed out of school, had children out of wedlock and in their teenage years, and have an attitude that someone else is to blame. Every one of the causes of poverty is subsidized by the central government for political reasons. The public education system is broken; the government undermines family, and the culture, and pays the poor for bad choices. Until we call it what it is we will continue to have the poor.

If we don't reduce the power of the central government we will all become poor but not the poor we see today. We have a choice to make and little time to make it. What we need is a return to self-reliance and the greatness we achieved through freedom and free markets. The federal government is subsidizing the cause of poverty and it must be stopped by returning to our founding principles...

THE POPE IS RIGHT AND WRONG... 9/24/2013

The Pope recently chided the world for the worshiping of "the God of money." The under tone of the comments were a criticism of capitalism. The Pope was right that worshiping money for the sake of money is to have an empty life. But the Pope was wrong when he said ""We don't want this globalised economic system which does us so much harm. Men and women have to be at the centre (of an economic system) as God wants, not money." "The world has become an idolator of this god called money," he said. This argument is too simple and could easily be heard by any two bit dictator of the world rousing the people's ire.

The greatest way to end poverty is to unleash the human desire to take care of one's self through the creation of products and services to be used by fellow humans. Capitalism is the answer to the world's woes. To say that the worker is the where we need to focus is wrong. We need to nurture the free exchange of goods and services by individual and every size business. When we nurture business we create jobs. When we create jobs we need workers. To say you support workers but demonize the people that create work is a circular argument that ends the same, no work or workers.

Money is not evil. The pursuit of money is not evil. Money is simply the mechanism used to exchange goods and services in a market. The more money you make the better off your circumstances. The Pope needs money to travel. Nothing is free. So the idea that the pursuit of money is the problem in the world is a really disingenuous argument to create envy among the people. The Pope seems to want to blame capitalism and the pursuit of money as the reason for poverty in the world. The reason for poverty in the world is government control of the economies of the poorest nations. Show me a poor country and I will show you a corrupt government. Socialist, communist, and dictatorships are the cause of poverty. Any attempt to control people and markets smothers the economy.

There are greedy people in the world and they are usually found in those corrupt governments. There are some captains of industry that are greedy but in America most contribute to the many charities and causes that help the less fortunate. It is their choice to do so and that is the way it should be. To take their hard earned money under the guise of "fairness" is the real greed. That is what corrupt governments do.

The Pope needs to be a promoter of capitalism around the world if he really wants to help the workers of the world. To stoke the fire of envy in the world is below the dignity of his position. The Catholic Church has a history of keeping property in the ownership of the Church. One of the many reasons Priests were forbidden to marry has roots in keeping property in the "family." In the 9th century priests that were married willed property to their wives and in 1123 celibacy was made was made official. Was that dictate out of greed? Why not share the accumulated property of the church? Why not sell the Vatican and its furnishings to give to the poor?

I am not trying to bash the Catholic Church. I was raised catholic and we had family friends that were priests. But the Pope needs to nurture the spirit of the human condition which is fed through freedom, the dignity of work and the ability to be compassionate. The most compassionate people are those that have succeeded through a capitalist economy. The Pope needs to support capitalism and the pursuit of a better life for all and that requires money...

ATTACKS ON SENATOR TED CRUZ... 9/26/2013

The people attacking Ted Cruz are foolish. The simple matter of fact is he is simply bringing attention to an issue that the American people are very concerned about, Obamacare. Obamacare is a disaster that will continue to have negative ramifications and may cause the collapse of the most powerful economy in the world.

You might expect democrats and the left to be on the attack because they are the ones responsible for voting for this destructive law, but republicans seem more animated about Ted Cruz than the democrats. In all honesty, there are probably many democrats that are silently praying this train wreck is stopped since it is an albatross around their necks in the next election. Democrats will not campaign on Obamacare because unlike in the 2012 presidential election, when it was still relatively unknown how this law would impact the average voter, today we see the millions of negative stories associated with Obamacare. So for Senator Chuck Schumer to say there was an election already on the merits of Obamacare that is disingenuous. No democrat will campaign on this unless they are in a safe leftist district. So why the republican ire?

The simple answer is that Ted Cruz is upsetting the leadership apple cart. He is forcing the republicans to take a principled stand. And if there is anything the current republican leadership is afraid of is a principled stand. The GOP leadership is all about power just like the democrats. That is also why they demonize the Tea Party. The GOP should be very careful how they treat the Tea Party. They are the reason that the GOP holds the majority in the house and could be the reason they gain the senate. But it may not work out that way in 2014 with the current crop of GOP incumbents.

So the GOP should remember that if their strategy is to win in 2014 they better stop insulting the base of the voters in the GOP. Attacking Senator Cruz is the same as attacking conservatives and Tea Party patriots. The GOP does that at their own peril. The conservative and Tea Party voters are principled and will put primary challengers in place or stay home in 2014. Some things are worth fighting for. Defunding Obamacare is one of those things...

MARKET BASED HEALTHCARE: A BRIEF THOUGHT...
10/01/2013

Every day in this country tens of thousands of businesses prepare the optimum amount of goods and services needed to efficiently serve the market. Dunkin Donuts bakes the right amount of donuts, restaurants prepare the right amount of soup and salad, and Walmart and thousands of other retailers stock the shelves with the right amount of inventory. Billions of transactions take place every day in the free market. Quality goods exchanged at a fair price. Why would we risk our most personal service needs, healthcare, to a government that can't even balance a budget? The people that push paper at the IRS have no business in your health care records or decisions. This is an absolute no brainer folks. This is too important to sit here and point fingers. This is OUR healthcare and we need to be in control; period!

A DISASTER SO EASY TO SEE... 10/10/2013

"If you think healthcare is expensive now, wait until it's free!" Ronald Reagan. In all his wisdom, Ronald Reagan would never suggest he was a man of exceptional intellect. He just used common sense. Albert Einstein never considered himself a genius; he simply was determined to use his God given gifts of intelligent exploration. We are all geniuses in our own right, but why are so many people blinded to the impending disaster of Obamacare?

Is it simply that people don't want to believe their government could be so incompetent? Do they dis-trust the private sector economy so much that the government seems to be a better choice with something as precious as healthcare? Do people not care? Are people too busy? There are probably many reasons why people are not willing to see this tragedy ahead for our healthcare, freedom, and country, but you don't need to be a genius to predict the results.

A simple look at history will give you all the reasons you need to be scared to death of centralized government. Especially centralized governments that say they have your best interests at their core. Ask the millions of people slaughtered by Stalin's government. Oh wait, you can't. Ask the millions of people killed by Pol Pot in Cambodia. Oh wait you can't. Ask the millions of people killed by Mao Ze-Dong of China. Oh wait you can't. And the list goes on. What do they all have in common? They all promised to "take care of the people" from some evil force or something. How could millions of people be fooled to support a government that so obviously has no capacity to take care of anything? What they also have in common is the belief that the "community" is more important than the individual.

Our US Constitution protects the individual from the government. We are an anomaly in the history of the world. The fact that our government is dependent on its power from the people is why we have enjoyed such prosperity and freedom throughout our short history. The fact that the free exchange of goods and services between groups and individuals has been free of government control is why we are successful. It is also why resources are abundant in America unlike the countries that I mentioned above, and the countries that have socialism (a system that claims to be "fair" to everyone equally) as their government structure, like Cuba.

If we follow the logic of Obamacare, does it look like a system that would be more comfortable in a communist/socialist country? Or in America where we have always believed in the free exchange of goods, services, and ideas between individuals?

Obamacare is about controlling cost, services, access, pricing, and delivery of healthcare. If a program is so good for the people it is supposed to serve, why does the government have to force people to join? Why is the government forcing doctors and hospitals to accept their payment schedules? Why is the government threatening people with fines and liens if this is supposed to be a system that helps the people? Things that are designed to help people don't need to force people under penalty of law to comply.

A truly effective healthcare system relies on the choices of individuals to utilize the services they believe are best for them. An effective healthcare system starts with doctors and hospitals creating services at a price people need and can afford. Healthcare is no different than shopping around for any other product or service we need. The cost of healthcare should be driven by what people can and are willing to pay without third party assistance. Third party payers are what have been driving up healthcare costs over the years. Costly and tightly controlled Medical Schools, the threat of mal-practice lawsuits, regulations that impede the free exchange of services have all played a role in driving up costs. And in every instance it is either government regulation or third party payers that are impacting costs negatively.

Doctors should get paid fairly for their services; hospitals should operate under their own business models, because in the end they need patients to pay their bills. The healthcare industry like every other industry needs to compete for the individuals business. Then and only then will prices reflect the true value of the service. We need more doctors and hospitals and fewer government programs, IRS agents, and laws that utilize force and coercion.

If we lose sight of the individual over the community, the individual becomes expendable. Group think is responsible for millions upon millions of tragic horror stories throughout history. Don't believe it can't happen in America because it will. When demand increases, supply is short, lines are long and doctors are few, who do you want determining whether or not you receive medical treatment, you or some government agent? Under Obamacare you will be expendable and that will be a tragedy.

If healthcare is given the freedom to operate in a free market, demand will level, supply will be abundant, lines will be non-existent, and you and only you will decide what healthcare services you need and want. We have a choice and the choice is clear. Even Albert Einstein and Ronald Regan could make this choice. It doesn't take a genius...

Now that is a lesson every young American should study...

LEADERS NEVER FOLLOW POLLS... 10/15/2013

If there were polls in the days of our founding we would have never had the blessings of liberty we take for granted today. Mike Huckabee on his radio show last night criticized the Tea Party Republicans because there was no way to "win" the defund Obamacare movement, so it was foolish to stand up against the law. He and many other conservative talk hosts have been crowing about the polls. The polls are not in support of shutting down the government to stop Obamacare, and the shutdown will hurt future elections! Polls are just snapshots of opinions at that time. They do not reflect changing circumstances because everything is fluid. And leaders change circumstances.

Thank God our founders were leaders and not the sheep we see today. Most people don't realize that the movement for our independence back in 1775 and 1776 was a minority movement. Most colonists were either supportive of the King, looking for a resolution that would keep the colonies part of Britain, and just a few visionaries could see the centralized authority of a King was an abuse of natural law. If a poll were taken at the time of our founders declaring independence - it would be at best 30% support. That means 70% of the country was eventually led to victory.

All throughout the revolutionary war, George Washington was outnumbered, fighting for support and supplies, and in many instances, at the breaking point of defeat. If the talk show hosts were around then, they would have been treating George Washington the same way they are treating Senators Cruz, Lee, and Paul. They would be spreading the criticism that we should wait until we can win. George should surrender since there was no way to win. They would be suggesting we must wait until we can convince enough people that the revolution is a good idea. "Just look at all the cannons and bullets they have" and we "have no hope!" These people are a bunch of comfortable talking heads that don't understand that this country is in real trouble.

A true leader takes the risk of taking the first step in the battle. This is a battle that CAN be won. Any leader knows if they can get the truth in front of the people, the polls will follow. So will the talk show hosts.

We are spiraling into debt, we have a President that is incompetent at best, and we have democrats in the senate that are left wing radicals and must be repelled and defeated. We have middle of the road republicans that are the new Gentry class and are too comfortable in being useless at governing but too incompetent to make it in the private sector.

Our founders were brilliant leaders, strategic geniuses, but most importantly they were men of character. They were willing to risk everything that was precious to them for the sacrifice of a better future for their posterity. Our "leaders' today borrow like thieves in the night from our future generations. It is time for every patriotic American to lead; the polls will follow...

DEAR POLITICIANS: IT'S HEALTHCARE NOT HEALTH INSURANCE, STUPID! 10/29/2013

Can we reset this entire healthcare argument to focus on the real issue here? The issue is healthcare not health insurance! This is driving me nuts. We don't go to the insurance company to diagnose our runny nose do we? We don't ask some insurance bureaucrat to reset our lower back due to a tweak we have after lifting a box the wrong way, do we? We don't go to the insurance office to get a prenatal exam during pregnancy, do we? NO we go to the doctor's office.

We have been so programmed to deal with insurance companies for healthcare issues that we can't see the forest through the trees. We should be dealing directly with our doctor to set up our appointments and make payments according to the services provided. Instead we are calling insurance companies to discuss co-pays and coverage of basic services that actually are already affordable.

Now we are on the cusp of adding government bureaucrats into the mix of insurance bureaucrats to get in the way of the relationship between us and our doctor. What are we nuts! The answer is not to empower more useless paper pushing or key banging office people to manage such a simple transaction. Just as you go to the mechanic to fix your car and then you pay the bill, you should be going to the doctor, receive your care, and pay your bill.

The biggest issue that drives the "need" for insurance is the fear of taking ill and needing critical or chronic long term care. The fear of bankruptcy is the biggest driver of insurance. Just like we fear fire and flood destroying our housing investment, in healthcare we fear a heart attack, a cancer diagnosis, or some other illness because if we don't have insurance it can bankrupt us! What if the issue of going bankrupt from a healthcare issue could be solved? How would that change the complexion of healthcare?

From the service provider side, doctors, nurses, and hospitals fear being sued for mal-practice. They have to carry mal-practice insurance which increases costs and does little for the betterment of healthcare. Actually it has created a "lottery" mentality where any "mistake" is treated as a ticket to Easyville! No doubt there are circumstances where doctors or hospitals are negligent, but lawyers have made an industry of suing doctors for every issue just to get in front of an ignorant jury that award large paydays. Most of the time these frivolous lawsuits are settled to reduce the time and effort it takes to fight the lawsuits. The way to fix it is to have jurists that understand medicine instead of the normal jury process. A "jury of your peers" in healthcare are people that understand healthcare, and I'm not suggesting this to put the fix in for doctors, but to put people on the jury that understand the complex arguments that we just are not educated to understand. It also would reduce the emotional component of "regular" jurists that end up awarding ridiculous amounts for things that are not malpractice. As healthcare professionals know, there is inherent risk in certain procedures. If we don't address this doctors will stop doing surgeries that have any risk and who benefits from that? What if mal-practice lawsuits were changed? How would that change the complexion of healthcare?

Eliminating insurance from preventative care, removing the fear of bankruptcy due to an illness, and mal-practice reform would be three steps that would change the face of healthcare for the better. If we did those three simple things to start we could then look at the market and see what other issues we could improve through free market principles.

The debate about healthcare should not be dominated by insurance but rather the improved delivery and management of healthcare. Oh and the biggest change of all: get politicians out of our doctor's office!

HEALTHCARE IS NOT A RIGHT... 10/31/2013

Rights are inherent and are common to all human beings. There are only God given rights, rights cannot be granted by government, but they can be taken away. When people talk about healthcare being a "right" the first question we must ask is: if healthcare is a right, then the people providing healthcare are slaves. Otherwise, it can't be a right. If a doctor or nurse is needed to provide healthcare then they can't be forced to provide the service of healthcare.

People use the term "rights" in a way that riles up crowds of malcontents who have been persuaded they deserve something for nothing. You could call that leftism, modern liberalism, communism, or socialism, you choose. The reality is we only have a few true rights as human beings. I believe those to be, freedom to move, freedom to believe or not, freedom to speak, right to our labor, right to private property, right to privacy, right to be left alone, and the right to contract with others. Every one of those rights has one thing in common; they don't rely on anyone else or expect something from anyone else.

Words mean things. When we use terms in society and politics it is important to use the proper terms. It is why the US Constitution was so brilliant. Just because healthcare is not a right, doesn't mean it isn't important. It doesn't mean as a society we shouldn't develop policies that help everyone to have access to good healthcare. We should use the same principles in healthcare as we do in other markets like the food industry where the growth and distribution have been able to feed the entire world. You can argue that food is just as important as healthcare. So why do we treat the distribution differently from the government perspective?

The federal government is not allowed to constitutionally do what it is doing in healthcare but it is because too many people are constitutionally illiterate, and we have a Supreme Court that has shunned its responsibility to protect it. We would be better off if we cut the funding for the federal government in half by going to a flat tax and eliminating the IRS, the Department of Education, Commerce, Energy, and Housing. That would leave plenty of money to provide for the poor and truly needy. At the state level we could decide what else we are willing to pay for as citizens. This way if we don't like the policies we can move to another state.

The way things are we have no place to go. The freedom to move is a right that is no longer relevant when the federal government controls things they shouldn't, like healthcare. Healthcare is not a right but it is too important to leave to an incompetent federal government...

A BIRTHDAY WISH... 11/03/2013

I believe the reason we celebrate birthdays, is to remind us that time is passing by. Time is very cunning; it silently slips past and makes no effort to remind us of the time we have let pass. How many times do we think about time in a way that places the value on it that it deserves?

Time is all we really have if you think about. And if you talk to someone in their later years you realize that even at the age of 96, the realization that time moved so fast changes nothing. What we need to realize is that in the time we have, building relationships that enrich our lives is the best legacy we can leave.

I volunteer at Hospice and I had a patient that grew up in the Bronx and met Babe Ruth as a kid. He used to take the train to 125th street in Harlem to see all of the great jazz players at the Apollo Theatre. What I learned as he told me his stories was that every story he told me was about the people he met and the family he loved. He had little interest telling me about his career, he would always turn the conversation back to the people and his family. His life's memories boiled down to wonderful stories about the people.

My mom died last year and when I think about the 75 years she was given, she spent most of it staying in touch with family and friends. She lived the life of a Saint because what drove her was to add value to everybody's life she came in contact with. Her legacy, when I tell stories about my mom, is about how she loved to connect with people. She never wanted to talk about herself; she wanted to know about the person she was talking to. It didn't matter to my mom whether you were the president or the superintendent of the building. She just wanted to learn more about the person she was talking to. She was always willing to help in any way she could.

The older we get the more we understand what is important. Birthdays remind us to refocus our efforts on the things that are important. The people in our lives, the dreams and goals we have are limited to the time we are given. We never know how much time we will be given so every Birthday gives us a day to think about what is important.

This birthday I am away for work. Today I was given the wonderful wishes of family and friends. Talking to my wife and children was the only gift I needed. And it is always a gift to have a loving family!

Since my last birthday 365 days have passed. I can't get any one of them back but I can tell you that they were not wasted. Most of those days were spent healthy, a part of a wonderful family, many camping trips, college visits, family visits, and many conversations with friends and family. I have a lot of goals and dreams as well. They are on track but they are also prioritized properly. Family first, always.

My wife Justine is a compassionate nurse that comforts family's at the most difficult times of loss. Taylor is an excellent student working hard to become a medical student. Emily is currently choosing colleges and has many choices because she works hard and is very smart. We have 3 pups that make every return home wonderful because they share their unconditional love that fills our hearts. These are the things that I am so proud to be a part of. A family is the legacy we leave. I couldn't be more proud of my family.

My Birthday Wish is that everyone takes a moment on their birthday to think about what is important. Tell someone you love them. Send a card to a friend that might be struggling. Hug that kid tighter tonight so they know how much you love them. Remember we are here for a limited time. Use every minute you can to let people know you care.

I have never been happier in my entire life because I have so many wonderful people in my life! I hope you can say the same! Happy Birthday!

WHY DO WE GIVE THANKS ON VETERAN'S DAY?
11/11/2013

This is the day we honor our veterans for their service to our country. It is a day that all political spectrums come together in thanks for the people that have served this greatest nation on earth. It is the greatest nation in a large part due to the strong desire there is in this country for freedom. We hold freedom as the most fundamental principle and right of every human being.

Every one of the founders of this nation was prepared to die for the cause; throwing off government control and creating the concept of self-rule. Up until that point it was the norm that government controlled people's lives, and that birth right was the way it would always be. If you were born of royalty, someday you would rule the kingdom. The founders turned that concept upside down and created the miracle we call the United States of America, and its founding principles the US Constitution.

The founders knew freedom wasn't free, and that it could only survive if the citizens were willing to fight, defend, and die for the cause. The founders expected a lot from the citizens and believed that once individuals were given freedom they would certainly be willing to defend that God given right. The founders believed in God and that certain rights were beyond the realm of man. They believed the rights to life, liberty, and the pursuit of happiness were precious and worth dying for.

The founders also knew that history was a great indicator of the future, and that human behavior had to be harnessed to protect those most basic rights. They harnessed them in limiting government and expanding individual freedom to the outer limits. They knew individuals could only prosper if they were allowed to freely create their path without government intervention. It worked for a hundred years. The last hundred years have been a return to the past that the founders were so intent on protecting us against.

Since FDR, we have seen a drift back to some utopian vision that the collective is more important than the individual. We have seen an expansion of government and a reduction in individual freedom as we have drifted away from the individual to a more powerful centralized government. If we look today it is such a stark contrast to our founding. A founding that took many lives in a revolution that changed the world. George Washington and his small band of troops set the example of how a powerful cause, freedom, could defeat the most powerful military in the world. He proved how individuals with a cause were the most powerful weapon in the fight for freedom. The spirit and hearts of the soldiers were more powerful than any mechanical weapon or fancy uniform.

Our military men and women have always answered the call to protect freedom. They have done miraculous things around the world and have been responsible for more freedom than any other entity in the world. These men and women are a shining beacon to others that when the cause is just, and the nation calls, they are willing to risk their lives, fortunes, and sacred honor. They leave friends and family behind in the cause of freedom and defense.

While this small minority of military veterans has sacrificed so much in the defense of freedom, we need to ask - have we done our part to honor that sacrifice? Have we protected those freedoms by electing people that honor our constitution and the cause of freedom? Have we been diligent in monitoring the policies that have given us such prosperity and opportunity for future generations? Would George Washington be proud to have sacrificed so many in the cause of freedom he so honorably gave to us?

We honor our military veterans today because they believe in the cause of freedom. They believe our freedoms are worth fighting and dying for. If we look at how intrusive and over reaching our central government has become we must ask – have we been staunch defenders of freedom as the citizens of this great nation?

I know our veterans have held up their part in the role of self-rule. We honor them today and thank them. But what I wish and believe honors our veterans the most is to do our part and protect our freedoms by engaging in the political process with the intensity our veterans have pursued theirs.

God Bless our veterans and their families!

WHY THE INCOME GAP IS A RED HERRING... 11/18/2013

Just say the rich are getting richer and the poor are getting poorer and you will find yourself surrounded by liberal and leftists salivating to tell you how bad capitalism is as an economic system. They trace the increase in this gap back to the Reagan years. There is no doubt that the income gap exists but what does it mean, and what are the causes?

If we look at the greatest expansion of wealth in this country for the most Americans ever, you find that expansion during the Reagan years. More people than ever were able to participate in the growing economy because of the massive job growth. This opportunity added to people being able to fund 401K's, buy homes, drive multiple cars, and in general build individual wealth. Family incomes increased and people were living the American Dream.

During this same period and beyond, many industrious Americans were building companies that created enormous wealth for many individuals. Many became the 1%'s; so often targeted for envy by the left. You see, when wealth creation happens some people do better than others. They are rewarded for their ideas through the market and can accumulate massive wealth which they can then use to create or invest in other economic opportunities. The people that also benefited from this wealth creation were the people that worked at all of these businesses that were created. As employees often do, they saw increases in their pay and may have bought a home and made some investments in their future. Many increased their possessions and chose to spend instead of save. That's what freedom means, the ability to do what you want with your private property.

So the 1%'s saw huge expansion of their wealth as they chose to continue to invest in the economy. Some won and some lost. You see, the 1%'s are not the same set of people that were there in the 80's or 90's. The 1%'s change just like people in the 50% go up and down in income level based on their choices and circumstances.

The income gap is measured by "household income." So if your household has two working members you are likely to have a higher income. If you are a single parent household, your income level is likely to be less.

The chart in this article shows a reduction in households in the income ranges of $35K - $99K. The lower and upper ranges have grown. So there are more rich and more poor which increases the "gap." But what it doesn't show is who is moving where and why.

The income gap can be the result of so many factors but moving to the lower income levels has nothing to do with people moving to the upper income levels. There are simply more people in this country that have not become rich (yet), and the people at the high income level are a very small group of people and not the same people at any given time.

The left wants you to infer that the rich are rich because they are keeping the rest of the people in the lower income category. They have gotten to where they are as a result of screwing other people. There are some of those but they are the people using political power to get and maintain wealth. They are the exception not the rule. This is the left's attempt to use envy as their weapon to destroy even more wealth.

The income gap proves nothing but the fact that some people have been better at creating wealth in the marketplace. The people moving into the lower income levels have many stories but they also have the opportunity to get back out of that group if the government would stay the heck out of the economy.

What the left wants to do to "fix" the gap is to reduce everyone's ability to succeed. They want to regulate wages, business opportunity, tax the rich, re-distribute according to the left's definition of fair. A "fair" that punishes success and rewards poor choices and the invisible hand of the market place.

Taking from the rich, increasing taxes, stealing people's hard earned retirement, and creating envy among people is evil and needs to be rejected by every American that still believes in the American Dream. There is the greatest gap in incomes where there is the most freedom. The people that are determined to succeed become wealthy. Some people are driven more than others and depending on choices some may be left behind by not creating any personal wealth. This is why freedom is so great and why so many on the left hate it! They hate it because it rewards based on merit. A free market does not care who you vote for, what color your skin is, what heritage you come from, it only cares if you have something everyone else wants. A true free market can't be manipulated by politics and that's what the left hates...

THE POPE IS WRONG... 11/26/2013

Pope Francis has the noble goal of ending poverty. But the Pope has the wrong solution; spreading socialism. In his first "position paper" as the Pope, he attacks the free market calling it a "new tyranny." This Pope may be popular but his thoughts on how to create the best opportunity for the poor is dangerous.

This Pope has grown up in an area of the world that is rich in resources but poor in access to those resources. The government in the name of "helping the poor" is doing the exact opposite. What socialists like the Pope fail to realize is the absolute truth of the Bible story "Teach a Man to Fish." Socialism is about punishing success. It takes away an individual's incentive to work hard because no matter how hard you work under socialism (unless you are a politician); you make the same as the guy who doesn't work at all.

Compassion is a great trait to have but not at the expense of other people's individual right to keep the harvest of their labor. It is easy to feel bad for the poor but it is exactly that feeling that destroys the poor's incentive to help themselves. Compassion should be measured by how many people can take care of themselves - not how many people the government supports through re-distribution programs.

The Pope talks about the unhealthy pursuit of money. But it is not money people pursue; it is the lifestyle that having money provides for the people that have money. Human nature is proven through history and a billion studies. Human nature defines the actions we take to survive and thrive. When we are incentivized with rewards, have the ability to create and keep wealth, we as humans then can focus on helping others. The United States is (although we are slowly losing the opportunity) the best example of compassion. Because we value individual wealth creation, our nation boasts of being the most charitable nation in the world. It is because of excess that we can be charitable. If our wealth is confiscated by governments, our ability and will to be charitable is diminished.

This Pope would do well to understand why people have been leaving his church in droves, especially in the United States. The lack of women in the priesthood, the bureaucracy and the lack of connection with the way the world works today are just a few of the reasons. I believe tradition is important but the tradition of who is allowed to lead in the church is a tradition that should end. It can't be defended and is the ultimate "good ol boys club." The patriarchal nature of the Catholic Church is a stumbling block to connecting with more and younger people. That is where the Pope should spend his time. But this is hard work and disruptive to the Church's empire. It would also help with his socialist message to divest of the wealth of the Vatican and all of its holdings by giving them directly to the poor.

I know it is easier, and accepted, by many progressives in the world to denounce capitalism, greed, and wealth but it is the wrong message to send. This Pope seems to like the role of playing the "regular guy" and God Bless him for getting out into the real world. But if he really looks around at the real world what he will find is the enemy of the poor is not money, capitalism, or wealth creation. It is an ignorance of the economic realities that create the greatest opportunity for the poor.

This Pope should be out there spreading the word that government creates more poor, socialism creates more poor, and the answer is individual accountability and opportunity that is the path to a healthy life. "Give a man a fish and he eats for a day, teach a man to fish and he can feed himself for life." Give the poor the wealth created by others and they soon become incapable of creating wealth for themselves. That serves no one, especially the poor...

IF YOU CARE DON'T ASK THE GOVERNMENT TO HELP...
12/09/2013

If you truly care about the needy, that last place you should look for assistance is a government agency. Government agencies and their perpetual quest to help the needy are the reason the numbers of needy have grown. Yet we still hear from seemingly educated people that we need the government to help.

I guess it's hard to understand that the government as a compassionate entity is hopeless. I think that people that put their faith in government fail to realize that it is not their wishful thinking that makes people compassionate, it is people with compassion and the willingness to spend their own time and money is what makes for compassion.

Too often liberal people want someone else to help the poor and that "someone else" for liberals is the government. Even when the evidence is clear that government is a failure at almost everything it does, why would we subject the needy to the workings of a failed government bureaucracy?

Detroit is a city that is the shining example of a place that embraced government intrusion in every aspect of the city's management. Chicago streets are the shining example of government programs designed to help minority youth in the city. NYC is the shining example of how government programs have chased many of the most successful from the city and if Wall Street financial firms ever decide to go to another city, it would be completely devastated. Public education is an absolute failure in DC, NYC, LA, Chicago, Houston, and every other major city in this country.

Black Americans have too often relied on government programs for their subsistence. I will only say that having grown up in the Bronx, I can tell you first hand, those government programs have created dependency and stolen the hope of multiple generations of Black Americans.

The healthcare system is being destroyed right before our eyes because of government tinkering and liberals still can't figure out that the place to put your faith is in yourself and the individual. It is not complicated.

I wish liberal people would stop trying to "help" others by asking the government to do what private citizens and civic and church groups are much better suited to do if you actually want to help the needy...

A POLITICAL CHRISTMAS WISH FOR AMERICA...
12/12/2013

I am tired of the assault the federal government has perpetuated on the people they are sworn to serve. The latest assault Obamacare, is the most dangerous assault in my lifetime. This healthcare takeover is not only unconstitutional (no matter what tortured logic John Roberts used to uphold it), it will cause the death of an unknown number of Americans. It is why I am praying hard for the following:

- I pray that we begin to see the fallacy that a government of the people, by the people, for the people can succeed without the moral foundation of a belief in God.
- I pray Americans wake up to the radical left wing that has taken over the former Democratic Party, and vote to elect constitutional supporters in the next election.
- I pray for all of the victims of Obamacare that have lost their insurance while fighting life threatening diseases. That their stories will end the federal government's takeover of healthcare. And mostly they find an alternative to continue to successfully fight their diseases.
- I pray that the State convention process under Article V of the constitution takes hold and passes term limits as its first successful amendment.
- I pray that every young adult is awakened to the assault on their future opportunity which is being destroyed by an out of control federal government - spending and borrowing away their future.
- I pray that the military and intelligence agencies are not as aloof as our president when it comes to monitoring

and stopping terrorists. And they stop spying on Americans because it is the right thing to do.

- I pray for the end of poverty by reducing government programs that remove incentives to be self-reliant.
- I pray that the capitalist system takes the Obamacare disaster and creates a better more efficient and compassionate alternative to healthcare.
- I pray that Americans wake up and realize politics does matter and that they have a direct role in ensuring a bright future for their children. And they do their due diligence on candidates and don't simply vote party lines.
- And finally, I pray the president and democrats are overwhelmed by the response of the American people and stop their assault on American tradition and values.

Merry Christmas! I pray that you and your family have health and happiness during this Christmas season and throughout your lifetime...

DUCK DYNASTY; THE TIPPING POINT? 12/19/2013

For far too long, a majority of Americans have been quietly ignoring small groups of malcontents that continue to push their agendas in the face of the people who may not agree with their views but are tolerant of allowing those views to be heard. Is the latest attack on Duck Dynasty patriarch Phil Robertson the final tipping point?

There comes a time when a bully is finally confronted by the victim and the outrage is so pent up that the results are rarely good for the bully. The American people's compassion and tolerance have been pushed by many. The atheists, the gay community, the democratic and republican big government types, race baiters, and the political correct coalition have all been pushing their agendas by belittling the majority of American's core beliefs...

The Duck Dynasty is a program that I have only watched once. I am not a huge TV guy. But it is the largest cable TV show in the history of cable. It is a family that lives by many of the core values the majority of Americans live by. At the end of every show they say a prayer and praise Jesus. That alone makes it a target of every politically correct group in the nation. But here's the problem, the cumulative number of politically correct groups in comparison to the majority of Americans are not worth comparing. But even though their numbers are small they have figured out how to drive the conversation in their favor.

Tolerance is not accepted by these minority groups. Their creed is: if you don't believe the way we do, you must be silenced and destroyed. That is not a core value of the Americans they are intent on destroying. A majority of Americans is truly tolerant and believe in free speech and liberty for all. But the groups they are tolerating do not want the majority to have those same courtesies.

The network A&E decided that comments made by Phil Robertson about his religious beliefs in a personal interview by GQ Magazine, and shared by a large majority of Americans, was an opportunity to punish him by firing him from his family's show. This may be the tipping point.

No matter how you feel about the comments made by Phil Robertson about the gay lifestyle, in America tolerance is how we best react to people's individual opinions. We don't have to agree and we especially don't have to watch the show, but to silence a man's opinion because a small militant group has decided this opinion is to be silenced, we must reject their actions.

It is time that the majority of Americans that are tired of being told their beliefs are no longer allowed to exist in America, fight back. We need to treat these small radical and intolerant groups the way they have been treating us for years. We need to shut them up by shutting them out of our concerns. We no longer should ignore their radical agenda and we must respond in numbers so overwhelming that these groups understand and everyone observing has no doubt, they are the minority opinion in America.

The attack against the religious beliefs of a member of the Duck Dynasty family may be the attack "heard around the world" by the overwhelming majority of the good tolerant people, no longer willing to ignore the assaults on their beliefs...

CONCLUSION

Nothing like closing on Duck Dynasty! I have only watched the program once and as you can tell the controversy is not about the show but about our ability as Americans to discuss important issues of the day. I love talking about the importance of politics because I believe it underpins everything America stands for. Without a strong political system that limits central control and empowers the individual we have nothing!

Most of my writing has some political component to it because of my love for people and this country. I look at country's that have all or more natural resources than we do here in the United States but are mired in abject poverty. Why is that? Why do some countries live a more blessed life than others? It is always tied to the political system they support in their country.

If you support socialism and central government you are damned to a life of common misery. If you value the individual and restrict central authority to a limited role, you thrive.

The country is in a major transition due to the lack of educational integrity in our public school system. We have raised too many generations of people that have no interest or knowledge in the history of our founding. It is a cancer that must be defeated with an injection of knowledge and a return to civics focused on the role our country has played in the betterment of this world. That is a huge and important curriculum to ensure our survival as a nation.

We can no longer stand by and watch people focus only on the negative aspects of our history. Every nation has negative events and we have some but nowhere near the other nations of the world. If you were to create two columns, one negative and one positive, there is no doubt the good we have done as a nation far outweighs any negatives.

We can't ignore the negative but we have as a nation improved because of these negative events. Not many countries can say the same.

I am proud of what America stands for and I am always going to defend the truth about our country. But I refuse to allow our country to be defined by people that hate us or harbor some kind of guilt complex. I am too smart for that and I believe most Americans are as well...

The beauty about this book is that it can be read like short stories. The only consistency is the timeline. It chronicles the political happenings and my thoughts of the past year, 2013.

I write because it makes me feel good and I definitely have something to say. But as I mention a few times in my first book My Life; Ignored! Life Is Too Short To Ignore Yours! I know this book and it's profound message will be mostly ignored!

In May of 2012 my Mom died. She was my biggest fan and I could always count on here for my first sale. I miss her and the wisdom she shared with me my entire life. It is why I dedicated it to her. Thanks Mom for never ignoring me!

About the Author

Rich Hand is a seasoned speaker, not only in his dreams but in reality as well. He has presented at numerous meetings and conferences. He is a song writer, musician, and has produced three CDs of original music. The father of two wonderful children and devoted husband of ~~two~~, I mean one wonderful wife that has been inspired by his books to write her own, *My Wife's Life: Ignored!* It should be a real gut buster! He has worked his way through life, from the "trash room" to the "board room." Never once did he doubt his destiny of becoming a New York Times best-selling author, but the road is not complete. He is still not a New York Times bestselling author, just an author. He asks you kindly to help him with his dream and read his books. He knows you will laugh, mostly at him, but his goal is to help you discover your true passion in life and take action to live that passion. He wants nothing more than to meet all the people in this world worth meeting. He has met some "famous" people in his life and has not been impressed. He wants to meet the people who are "famous" by his new definition of the term, and to hear the stories of those that truly make it a worthwhile endeavor on this earth. Be one of them by reading this book!

My Life; Ignored! Life Is Too Short To Ignore Yours!
The Teenager's Guide to Life, Liberty, and the Pursuit of Happiness: A Parent's Gift!
My Blog; Ignored! Write Because You Have Something To Say!
My Music; Ignored! Behind Every Song There Is A Story & A Dream!
The Shortest But Most Effective Book To Improve Customer Experience Delivery!
The Professional Association: Cultivating Leaders and Harnessing the Power of Community

www.ingramcontent.com/pod-product-compliance
Lightning Source LLC
Chambersburg PA
CBHW060424290526
45791CB00002B/866